FINANCE AND THE INTERNATIONAL ECONOMY

3

The prize-winning essays from the first two competitions have been published in the following Oxford University Press volumes:

Finance and the International Economy (the 1987 Essays)
eds. John Calverley and Richard O'Brien

International Economics and Financial Markets (the 1988 Essays)
eds. Richard O'Brien and Tapan Datta

Finance and the International Economy

3

The AMEX Bank Review
Prize Essays

In Memory of
Robert Marjolin

Edited by

RICHARD O'BRIEN and INGRID IVERSEN

PUBLISHED BY OXFORD UNIVERSITY PRESS

For The AMEX Bank Review

1990

Oxford University Press, Walton Street, Oxford OX2 6DP

Oxford New York Toronto
Delhi Bombay Calcutta Madras Karachi
Petaling Jaya Singapore Hong Kong Tokyo
Nairobi Dar es Salaam Cape Town
Melbourne Auckland
and associated companies in
Berlin Ibadan

Oxford is a trade mark of Oxford University Press

Published in the United States
by Oxford University Press, New York

British Library Cataloguing in Publication Data

Finance and the International Economy, 3, The
AMEX Bank Review prize essays: in memory of Robert
Marjolin.
1. International financial markets
I. Marjolin, Robert   II. O'Brien, Richard, 1950–
III. Iversen, Ingrid   IV. The AMEX Bank Review; 0265-945X
332
ISBN 0–19–829008–X

Library of Congress Cataloging in Publication Data

Finance and the International Economy, 3, The AMEX bank Review
prize essays in memory of Robert Marjolin / edited by Richard
O'Brien and Ingrid Iversen.
Bibliography: p.
1. International economic relations.   2. International finance.
3. Marjolin, Robert.   I. Marjolin, Robert.   II. O'Brien, Richard.
III. Iversen, Ingrid.   IV. The AMEX bank Review.
HG1359.I585   1990   337   dc20   89-31876
ISBN 0–19–829008–X

Set by Oxford Text System
Printed in Great Britain by
Biddles Ltd.,
Guildford and King's Lynn

The AMEX Bank Review Awards
In Memory of Robert Marjolin

The AMEX Bank Review Awards are given annually in memory of Professor Robert Marjolin, the first head of the OECD (at that time the OEEC) and Vice-President of the European Commission for the first ten years of the European Community's existence. Professor Marjolin was one of the key architects of the Community and instrumental in establishing international economic co-operation in the post-war period. From 1975 to 1986 he was Editorial Adviser to *The AMEX Bank Review*. The Awards were launched in 1987 to promote new writing and analysis on current international economic and financial issues.

The Awards are judged by a special committee, which in 1989 included: *Professor Raymond Barre*, former Prime Minister of France and former Vice-President of the European Commission; *Lord Roll of Ipsden*, President of S. G. Warburg Group plc; *Professor Peter Kenen* of Princeton University; *Bruce MacLaury*, President of the Brookings Institution, Washington DC; *Bahram Nowzad*, Chief Editor of the International Monetary Fund; *Kevin Pakenham*, Chief Executive of the London investment group, John Govett & Co. Limited; and *Richard O'Brien*, Chief Economist of American Express Bank Ltd. and Editor of the *Review*. Both Mr MacLaury and Mr Pakenham are Editorial Advisers to the *Review*. The Bank is most grateful for the major contribution of the committee members in judging this competition and for their assistance in the editing of this volume.

Robert Marjolin was one of the most distinguished European economists and public servants of his generation. He was a very practically minded economist, being more interested in achieving progress than advocating any one particular economic theory or dogma. In 1989 the English language edition of Robert Marjolin's memoirs, under the title *Robert Marjolin: Architect of European Unity*, was published by Weidenfeld and Nicolson. As *The Economist* writes in its review of these memoirs,

Robert Marjolin is a name that will ring bells in many people's minds but come into focus in few of them. Intellectually too honest either to be a forceful politician or to have the unreasonable convictions that take men to fame, he remained an *eminence grise* in postwar Europe.

For our part we would like to record our appreciation of Robert Marjolin's wise and friendly advice which was a constant encouragement in attempting to interpret current economic events.

The 1989 Competition

The year 1989 was the third year of the competition, and 293 economists from sixty countries entered, a record number. Essays, of no longer than 5,000 words, are on any subject in international economics of current relevance to financial markets.

Eleven prizes were awarded in 1989, of a total value of US $56,000. The awards for the first three essays were US $25,000, US $10,000, and US $5,000 respectively, with eight Special Merit Awards of US $2,000. The full version of the First Prize essay was published in the *Review*'s Special Paper series, no. 17, alongside abstracts of the Second and Third Prize essays. Authors of the first 100 essays were awarded a special presentation copy of the memoirs of Robert Marjolin.

The 1989 results were announced at a special presentation dinner in the City of London, on 16th November 1989. The awards were presented by the Rt. Hon. Robin Leigh-Pemberton, the Governor of the Bank of England and by Robert A. Savage, President and Chief Executive Officer of American Express Bank Ltd. Professor Raymond Barre delivered a short address on behalf of the award committee, following the presentations.

The competition continues in 1990 under the same terms and conditions and we look forward to another high quality level of entry, to make the awards a worthy memorial to the work of Robert Marjolin.

The Editors

Contents

Editors' Introduction

This book contains the full text of the eleven prize-winning essays in *The 1989 AMEX Bank Review* Awards, the essay competition in international economics and finance run by American Express Bank Ltd. in memory of Professor Robert Marjolin. The *Review* is the monthly international economics and financial publication of the Bank and is published in London.

It would not be much of an exaggeration to say that the collection provides a comprehensive and valuable set of analyses on the role of capital in the three main areas of international economic debate in the late twentieth century. The *first* group of essays tackles the key issues arising from the large payments imbalances between industrial countries. The *second* group analyses the impact of capital flows on developing countries and on the development process itself. The *third* group examines the role of markets in the two largest centrally planned economies. The essays range from those providing a broad discursive treatment of their subject, to those which present, in a very readable form, the results of detailed economic research. Perhaps most importantly for promoting debate, each essay draws out specific conclusions of relevance to policy-makers or the market-place.

Payments Imbalances, Exchange Rates, and Globalization

The first group begins with two contrasting essays debating the sustainability of international payments imbalances. In the First Prize essay, *John Makin* of the *American Enterprise Institute* argues that, counter to a great deal of current thinking, the large payments 'imbalances' of the major economies represent a rational response to the specific events in the 1980s, notably deregulation, increased economic integration, and the rise in relative wealth outside the United States. As a result, the large external deficits of the USA can be financed to a much greater extent than is often believed. He argues that since most of the dollar intervention has been sterilized, the large 'imbalances' and pressure for restrictive trade practices will persist. But he warns that it would be a serious mistake to 'manage trade' to try and close the payments gaps.

In contrasting style, the Second Prize essay, by *Giorgio Gomel* of the *Banca d'Italia*, delivers a more cautious message on the impact of the build-up of US foreign debt which derives from its persistent external deficit. Because the USA borrows in its own currency, it will be the unwillingness of lenders to incur further dollar risk, rather than assessment of US credit-worthiness, which will limit the financing of the US deficit. He suggests that a further dollar exchange rate fall may have to occur to induce foreigners to increase their holdings of dollars. Meanwhile, the fluctuation of the dollar's exchange rate may, over time, reduce the international investment role of the US currency.

The third and fourth essays in this group (both recipients of Special Merit Awards) take a narrow and a wide perspective, respectively, on the topic. *Robert Feinberg*, of *The American University*, reports on his new statistical work on the relationship between swings in the dollar's exchange rate and US prices. In particular he investigates why studies show relatively low 'passthrough' of exchange-rate changes into US inflation. His research concludes that this low observed passthrough results, to a significant degree, from the use of inappropriate measures of the changes in the dollar's exchange rate. In particular he recommends that analysts should focus on the wide, 101-country index published by the Federal Reserve Bank of Dallas rather than the narrower, ten-country index published by the Federal Reserve Board. He also suggests that if greater attention is given to more industry-specific indices of the exchange rate, some US manufacturers would be seen to be much less competitive than is recognised.

In contrast, *Paul Mortimer-Lee* of the *Bank of England* draws a broader sweep across the effect of financial market globalization on economic policy-making. The essay concludes that globalization of financial markets will lead to a closer convergence of economic policies but that formal co-ordination is not necessary as a well-functioning market should fill that role.

Finance and Developing Countries

The second group of essays provide five interrelated insights into the role of foreign capital in developing countries. The Third Prize essay, by *William Cline* of the *Institute for International Economics*, focuses on the debt crisis itself, and the two major US initiatives to solve it, the Baker Plan and the Brady Plan. Originally written for the competition in early 1989 but now with a short postscript, the essay stresses that while the Brady initiative on LDC debt reduction was a welcome move, debt reduction must not be forced on private lenders. To be successful, the initiative also requires more official resources to be made available. In his postscript, the author sees the progress made so far on a debt reduction deal for Mexico as a positive indication that other such arrangements may be negotiated for other selected borrowers. While the essay agrees that debt reduction is important, it also concludes that sound economic policies by debtors still hold the key to economic recovery, a conclusion shared by *Przemyslaw Gajdeczka* and *Daniel Oks*, of the *IMF* and the *World Bank* respectively, in their investigative essay on capital flight, economic policy, and debt. Their analysis seeks to link the incidence of capital flight with the flows of private bank-lending and economic policy in borrowing countries. The authors conclude that the return of financial flows into debtor countries depends heavily on the restoration of confidence in borrowing countries' economic policies and in their governments. This essay and the rest of the essays in this collection received a Special Merit Award.

The next essay examines the link between capital controls and economic development, within the framework of modern portfolio theory. *World Bank* economist *John Nash* emphasizes the very high economic cost of restricting long-term capital flows. He argues that if domestic savers are allowed to invest abroad this would enable them, and the economy, to help offset the risks deriving from the instability of export earnings. Foreign investors would also be able to assume some of the risks, but this requires restrictions on inward investments to be absent. By freeing capital movements, he argues, developing countries will be better able to escape from the traditional problem of dependence on unstable export earnings.

The final two essays on developing countries develop the links between external capital, the private sector, and economic policies pursued by developing country governments. *Cory Highland* of the *OECD Secretariat* focuses on the increasing efforts to ensure that official aid supports private sector development. He suggests that this effort should pay greater attention to the encouragement of favourable business conditions and to support adjustment and reform rather than specific projects. *Jeffrey Herbst* of *Princeton University* focuses on the experience in Africa, and in particular stresses that if debt relief is to help, relief should be conditional on the application of good economic-policy reforms. If the link is not made then debt reduction could have the unintended effect of removing the incentive for economic reform. Without external pressures, domestic political incentives tend to favour the continuation of poor policies rather than reform.

Reform in Centrally Planned Economies

Centrally planned economies are now seeking to enhance economic growth through the greater use of markets. In China this process began over a decade ago, on a limited basis, but in 1989 suffered a serious setback. *Davin Mackenzie*, of *Strategic Planning Associates*, uses the experience of China in developing its stock markets as his analytical vehicle for examining the economic reform process (the essay was written before the events of Tiananmen Square). Although stock markets often play a limited role in development (and even in major industrial economies are often very small) the essay provides a clear insight into the recent development of China's economy. In contrast, the Soviet Union is just beginning its efforts to embrace market practices. However, *Stephen Gardner* and *Steven Green* of *Baylor University*, Texas, warn that convertibility of the Soviet rouble will be long delayed given the extent of the economic reform task facing the Soviet Union. The authors conclude that not only is convertibility of the rouble a long way off, to attempt such convertibility now would have disastrous effects.

Essay Selection

These essays were chosen from 293 entries from sixty countries. Naturally it was not possible to reward all the entrants for their substantial efforts, but the next best 100 essays received a presentation copy of the newly released English translation of the memoirs of Robert Marjolin.

Initial scrutiny of the entries was conducted by the editors of the *Review*, with a short-list being submitted to the full Award Committee. In the selection process the judges were looking for several characteristics in the essays. Of particular importance was the extent of new thinking or research provided by the essays, though well-written essays bringing together more familiar but complex issues also fared well in the judging process. Stress was also placed upon the ability of authors to draw out clear conclusions and recommendations from the analysis. While selection involves a great deal of comparative judgement of the essays, each essay was reviewed on its own merits and on an anonymous basis with respect to authorship.

Editorial Notes

All the essays are published in the form in which they were submitted to the competition, with only minor changes. Short editors' introductions and author-biographies are presented with each essay. Many of the authors provide extensive references and footnotes: we have sought to ensure that the notes intrude as little as possible on the flow of the essays. A number of suggestions were given to authors by the judges, but authors have been left to incorporate all suggestions as they saw fit. We would like to thank all the authors for preparing their essays for publication very quickly, so that the collection could appear soon after the announcements of the Awards. We would also like to acknowledge the assistance of our colleagues Sarah Delo, Allison Fitz-Earle, and William Nye in preparing the book for publication. We are of course very pleased that all the essays continued to be published by Oxford University Press.

We hope that the essays will provide stimulating reading on current issues in international economics and finance and, not least, encourage the submission of a further set of high quality entries, by scholars, public officials, and private sector practitioners for the 1990 competition.

Richard O'Brien, Chief Economist
Ingrid Iversen, Economist
American Express Bank Ltd.

International 'Imbalances': The Role of Exchange Rates

FIRST PRIZE

Editors' Introduction

This essay by John Makin of the American Enterprise Institute, winner of the First Prize in the competition, argues that the large international payments imbalances of the 1980s, that have not been corrected despite large currency fluctuations, can be explained by an unusual combination of events in this period. The events of the 1980s which have led to the imbalances include deregulation, increased integration of the world economy, and the rise in relative wealth outside the USA. The author concludes that the resultant large net excess demand for US assets has allowed the USA to finance its large current account deficits.

An important part of the author's case derives from his demonstration that wealth outside the USA has grown so large that gross saving flows in major industrial countries are more than three times the US level. So far in 1989 the resulting net capital inflow to the United States has been at a $170 billion annual rate composed of a $120 billion offset to the current account deficit and a $50 billion offset to central bank dollar sales. He argues that, viewed in this way, a strong dollar in the presence of the large current account deficit is not a mystery. Since most of the dollar selling intervention has been sterilized, the large international 'imbalances' and attendant pressure for restrictive trade practices will likely persist.

The author stresses that restrictive trade practices should be resisted: that not only are they damaging to world trade but that it is not proven that the current levels of imbalances are in fact unsustainable. He concludes with the warning that the response to trade imbalances in a climate of greater freedom for capital movement should be to continue to promote free trade, not to try to 'manage' it.

John H. Makin, 46, is a resident scholar and Director of Fiscal Policy Studies at the American Enterprise Institute for Public Policy Research, Washington, DC. Earlier, he was a professor of economics and Director of the Institute for Economic Research at the University of Washington. He has written numerous books on fiscal policy issues, including *U.S. Fiscal Policy: Its Effects at Home and Abroad* (1986) and *Real Tax Reform: Replacing the Income Tax* (1985). He is a member of the Congressional Budget Office's Panel of Economic Advisers, serves as an associate editor of Harvard's *Review of Economics and Statistics*, and is Chairman of the Japan–United States Friendship Commission. He received his Ph.D in economics from the University of Chicago.

1

International 'Imbalances': The Role of Exchange Rates

JOHN H. MAKIN

Introduction

The 1980s have witnessed both large exchange rate movements and large persistent international imbalances. The coexistence of these events has produced dissatisfaction and discomfort both in academic and policy-making circles, though concern among the latter has been greater. Some have suggested that the persistence of imbalances is due to a changed world where exchange rates no longer 'work' to eliminate imbalances. Others have claimed that the persistence of large imbalances even after large exchange rate changes have occurred is *de facto* evidence of unfair trade practices. It is undoubtedly true that a new, more aggressive American trade bill would not have emerged in 1988 without the steady growth of the American trade deficit from 1981 until 1987.

There have been efforts by Dornbusch (1988), Hooper and Mann (1989), Krugman (1988), and Sachs (1988), to mention only a few, to consider the possibility that the unusual behaviour of exchange rates and external imbalances is a product of unusual exogenous events. More specifically, there has been considerable effort expended upon systematic explorations of observable changes in real and nominal exchange rates, and net external flows of goods and capital and their relationship to unusually divergent fiscal policies, changes in regulations affecting capital flows, wealth redistributions among industrial countries, and the effects of pegging the dollar at an overvalued level such as occurred in mid-1987.

It is odd that, in the presence of considerable analytical and empirical evidence that the co-movements of exchange rates and external imbalances are natural counterparts of identifiable exogenous events and differences in the responsiveness of international movements of goods and capital to changes in income, interest rates, and exchange rates, large segments of the policy-making community have chosen to conclude that the persistence of imbalances is *de facto* evidence that something is 'wrong' with the trading system. In fact, today's 'imbalances' as they are erroneously labelled are neither unusual nor indicative of a special unresponsiveness of behaviour to exchange rates coupled with rising protectionism. They are, therefore, not sufficient reasons to contemplate either 'managed trade', now so fashionable in Washington (see Kissinger and Vance, 1988, and Prestowitz, 1988), or a new exchange rate regime. Rather we should be reminded again of the importance of several things that we have known all along. Co-ordination of fiscal policy among industrial countries is important if large swings in exchange rates and external imbalances are to be avoided. The imbalances are not bad *per se* but they may lead to bad policies, including increased trade friction and resulting additions to existing impediments on the international flows of goods and capital.

Another lesson of the 1980s is the need to expect behaviour of exchange rates and international imbalances that are unusual by historical standards to result from exogenous events that are unusual by historical standards. Continued deregulation and increasing integration of global capital markets and production facilities, coupled with a sharp relative rise in real wealth outside the United States have resulted in a sustainable large net excess demand for US assets that manifests itself currently in a persistent US capital inflow of over \$100 billion, with the attendant persistence of current account and merchandise trade deficits.

It is important to avoid a misreading of the significance of such persistent 'imbalances'. They are not, when viewed in the context of global portfolio behaviour, imbalances, but rather sustainable flows that reflect the generation of intertemporal gains from trade. As such they do not manifest a failure of exchange rates to 'work', or indicate the persistence of unusually high barriers to trade. Therefore I shall refer hereafter to 'imbalances' in quotation marks to indicate a word frequently used incorrectly to characterize non-zero international flows of goods or capital. Though these views may seem unconventional to some, they are no more than an articulation in the unusual setting of the 1980s of the tautology that the balance of payments always balances. It is *how* it balances, especially when large capital flows are balanced against opposing large current account flows with attendant growth of external debt, that makes some observers uneasy.

Greater perspective and an understanding of the unusual combination of events governing international flows and exchange rates during the 1980s may help to dispel the tension that surrounds the question of the sustainability of such flows, and reduce the temptation to 'do something' in response.

The danger of damaging unilateral trade measures should be reduced by two other considerations: the fact that adjustment of America's external deficit is already underway, and the fact that the American Congress, currently in a mood to alter the tax code, could alter the tax treatment of interest income and expense so as to increase net saving by an amount sufficient to eliminate the American current account deficit while simultaneously achieving a widely sought increase in the American private saving rate (see Makin, 1989).

Section 1 reviews the recent history of exchange rate behaviour and international 'imbalances'. Section 2 examines the results of poor international fiscal policy co-ordination coupled with reduced restraints in Japan and Europe on capital outflows, and their effects on exchange rates and international imbalances. Section 3 considers the sustainability of international imbalances in the light of prospective portfolio behaviour by investors outside the United States where wealth is growing rapidly. Section 4 presents some concluding remarks.

1. Exchange Rates and External 'Imbalances'

Judged by the criterion that exchange rate adjustments should eliminate international imbalances, the floating exchange rate era since 1973 has been a failure. There have been over the past fifteen years very large changes in exchange rates, especially real exchange rates, accompanied by large, persistent, international 'imbalances'.

In addition to persisting exchange rate volatility simultaneous with large international 'imbalances', confusion has emerged about whether external 'imbalances' cause exchange rates to change or whether exchange rates cause changes in external 'imbalances'.

Take the United States, for example. The late 1970s saw the merchandise and current account deficits rise as the dollar fell. There was a tendency to emphasize the line of causation running from trade deficits to exchange rates, with the rising deficit taken as a sign that the dollar had to depreciate further.

The 1980s has seen both the sign of the exchange rate–deficit relationship and the suggested direction of causation reversed. As the dollar strengthened after 1980, the United States trade and current account deficits grew. The suggested line of causation ran from exchange rates to deficits. After early 1985 the dollar began to fall while US external deficits continued to rise for two more years.

The notion that the fall of the dollar had something to do with concerted policy actions initiated at the famous September 1985 Plaza Agreement arose in part from the fortuitous timing of the Plaza meeting approximately six months after the dollar had already begun to fall on its own. The dollar's weakness after the Plaza meeting was accentuated by tighter monetary policy in Japan during the autumn of 1985 and easier US monetary policy during 1986.

The February 1987 Louvre Accord was meant to suggest that the dollar had fallen far enough. It was, as it turned out, premature. The dollar was pegged at an overvalued level during mid-1987, and all of the pressure to achieve an equilibrium in international capital and commodity markets was thrust upon US real interest rates. By October 1987, US real interest rates had risen so sharply that investors stampeded out of stocks and into bonds.

After peaking in 1987, US external deficits in 1988 fell by about 20 per cent, partly as a result of behaviour associated with a sharp 40–50 per cent depreciation of the dollar (both in nominal and real terms) from its 1985 peak and partly due to tighter US monetary policy after April 1988. By early 1989 analysts were again expressing disappointment that the American merchandise trade deficit appeared 'stuck' at about $10.5 billion per month. Others, including Martin Feldstein (1988), argued that the dollar had to depreciate further to below 100 yen per dollar to reach 'sustainable' levels. The error of Feldstein and others including Bergsten *et al.* (1987) and Marris (1985), has been to suppose that the American external deficit must rapidly approach zero in order to be sustainable. As events of 1989 have shown, the dollar can even appreciate in the presence of sizeable US trade / current account deficits and heavy dollar-selling by central banks.

Against this background, which at times seems immensely confused and confusing to nonspecialists, and perhaps to specialists as well, there has emerged an uneasy tension surrounding global external accounts. The 1980s, and especially the period since the Louvre Accord early in 1987, have been very hard on the notion that only zero international 'imbalances', or at least less-than-three-digit international 'imbalances' constitute 'sustainable' equilibria. Since exchange rates have moved a lot while external 'imbalances' have moved only a little, 'practical' men and women have begun to ask if exchange rates 'work' any more.

It is obviously important to dispel confusion about the role of exchange rates in creating or eliminating international 'imbalances'. If exchange rates and international deficits or surpluses along with interest rates, incomes, and prices, are all viewed as endogenous variables instead of as some separate policy-instrument combination, rationalizing the events of the floating exchange rate era becomes much easier.

2. Deregulation of Capital Flows and Divergent Fiscal Policies

During the 1970s and 1980s there were significant reductions in the constraints on international capital flows that brought industrial countries outside the United States closer to the unregulated environment in the United States (see discussions by Fukao and Okina, 1988, Makin, 1986, 1988, and Koo, 1987). The United Kingdom abolished all exchange controls late in 1979. Since enacting a new foreign exchange control law in December 1980, Japan has steadily reduced restrictions on foreign investment by Japanese institutional investors. The history of Japanese relaxation of controls on overseas investment by institutional investors is plotted in Figure 1 against the annual level of capital flows from Japan to the United States.

In a world of capital mobility and rapid relaxation of constraints on capital outflows from large, rapidly growing economies like Japan and the rapidly diversifying economies of Japan and Europe, movement toward an external equilibrium need not coincide with a reduction in net flows of goods or securities between nations. Large and rising capital outflows from these economies have been mirrored by large inflows to the United States as a major trading partner of countries whose restrictions on capital outflows have been reduced.

At any given time, a general external equilibrium in the world

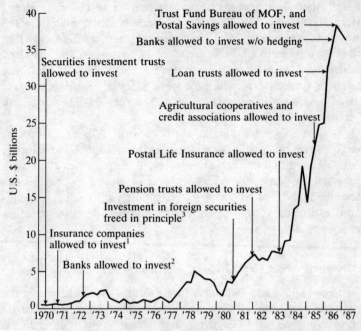

Figure 1. Deregulation of foreign securities investment
Source: Richard C. Koo, 'Japan and International Capital Flows', Nomura Research Institute, Tokyo, October, 1987.

trading system under any exchange rate regime may coincide with large offsetting net sales of financial assets and commodities. More specifically, the United States during the 1980s has been in equilibrium as a net seller of financial assets and a net buyer of commodities while Japan and other industrial countries have been in equilibrium as net sellers of commodities and net buyers of financial assets.

Viewed in this way, the usual characterization of 'massive' United States trade and current account deficits mirroring 'massive' Japanese surpluses, is instead replaced by an intertemporal exchange yielding intertemporal gains from trade on terms agreeable to all of the (private) parties involved.

This process was set in motion, given the relaxation of restrictions

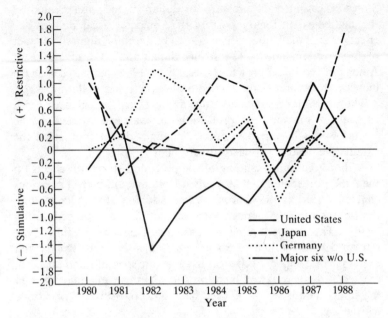

Figure 2. Change in structural budget balance, inflation adjusted 1980 to 1988
Source: OECD Economic Outlook, various issues.

on international flows of capital pursued by industrial countries outside the United States, by the emergence of immense pressure on exchange rates, generated by divergent fiscal policies being pursued by the United States relative to some other large industrial countries (see Makin, 1988).

More specifically, the 1980s were a period of fiscal retrenchment for most large industrial countries other than the United States. In the seven largest OECD economies public expenditure had risen from 33 per cent of GDP in 1972 to 41 per cent of GDP in 1982. But by 1982 the OECD's measure of government financial balances indicated a sharply expansionary policy in the United States, a neutral posture in Japan, and a strongly contractionary posture in Germany (see Figure 2). In the following two years, the American posture remained sharply expansionary while Japan's posture turned contractionary and the German posture remained contractionary, though slightly less so.

The broad pattern of fiscal retrenchment outside the United

States exacerbated the pressure for dollar appreciation created by the highly expansionary posture of American fiscal policy. The effect outside the United States was to cushion the domestic impact of fiscal retrenchment. The strong dollar and the rapid pace of American economic growth, especially in 1984, permitted a sharp increase in exports to the United States and other dollar areas.

The pressure on exchange rates and external 'imbalances', with subsequent pressure for protectionism, was exacerbated in the United States by micro tax policy changes that accompanied the stimulative posture of macro fiscal policy.

A thorough understanding of the profound structural effects on the American economy that resulted from tax and budget measures enacted in 1981 and 1982 provides a broader basis for understanding the origins of the American trade legislation that emerged during 1986-8. The microeconomic tax changes effected by the 1981-2 tax reform acts in the United States, coupled with the budgetary and exchange rate impact of changes in aggregate spending and taxation, created a dangerous combination for American manufacturers in the traded goods sector that fed back onto pressure for new trade legislation.

The major structural or microeconomic feature of the 1981-2 tax acts was a sharp reduction in the marginal effective tax rate on new investment. This was accomplished by liberalization of accelerated depreciation allowances along with investment tax credits that amounted to partial expensing allowances for qualified investments. Such measures sharply reduced marginal effective tax rates on income from new investments. In some cases, equipment investments in particular, marginal effective tax rates were negative.

The positive impact on new investment of the tax incentives put in place during 1981-2 was delayed by the recession of 1982. By late 1983, private investment in the United States accelerated rapidly just as the federal budget deficit was beginning to rise as well. The result was a sharp increase in overall American expenditure that was not matched by an increase either in government tax revenues or private saving.

The sharp increase in American absorption was accommodated on unusually easy terms by a large increase in lending from abroad. This was due partly to continuing relaxation of controls on capital outflows in Japan and elsewhere, and partly to the attraction of a rapidly growing US economy in which it appeared that inflation

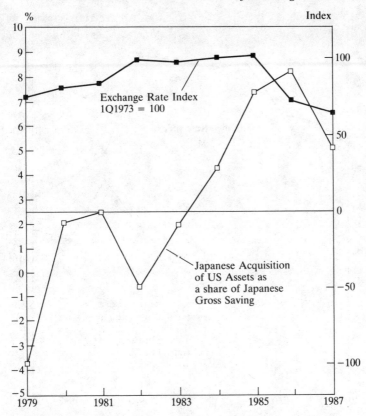

Figure 3. Exchange rates and Japanese acquisitions in US
Source: OECD and Bureau of Economic Analysis, US Dept. of Commerce.

was being brought under control. The share of foreign gross saving (OECD measure of gross saving in Japan, Germany, France, Canada, and Britain) directed to the United States rose from 11.4 per cent in 1983 to over 19 per cent in 1986 while the dollar appreciated in real terms by nearly 20 per cent (see Figure 3). Real dollar appreciation against the yen was nearly 40 per cent while the share of Japanese gross saving directed to the United States rose from 1.96 per cent ($7 billion) in 1983 to 8.2 per cent ($52 billion) in 1986 (see Figure 4).

The problem for American traded goods industries lay in the sharp appreciation of the dollar that accompanied the surge in private investment and government spending during 1983–4. Many

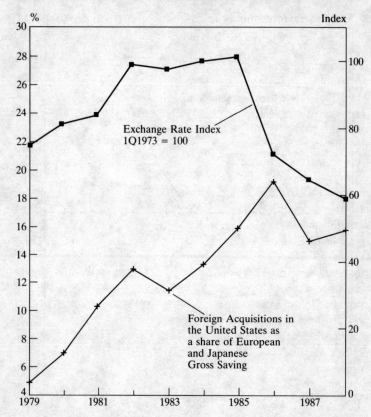

Figure 4. Exchange rates and foreign acquisitions in USA.
Source: OECD and Bureau of Economic Analysis, US Dept. of Commerce.

of the American companies that responded to the investment incentives in the 1981-2 tax acts found that they were unable to sell the goods produced with new stocks of capital when faced (both in domestic and foreign markets) with competition from goods produced abroad. In effect, the failure to anticipate the sharp appreciation of the dollar implicit in the unusual configuration of American fiscal and monetary policies and the accompanying retrenchment of fiscal policies abroad, caused American investors to over-invest in traded goods industries. As a result, by 1985-6, much of the new addition to the capital stock in the United States had been rendered economically redundant because of a sharp appreciation of the dollar.

The American economy in 1985 was really two economies. The non-traded sector was prospering thanks to the stimulative effects of a surge in government and private spending. The traded or manufactured sector was saddled with heavy excess capacity and an inability to compete in American and world markets (see Frankel, 1985 for further discussion of the 'two economies' theme). The sharp depreciation of the dollar after 1985 shifted demand onto the traded goods sector. With its fortuitous accumulation of new capital, America's traded goods sector was able to increase output without raising prices. The result was an unusually long economic recovery that became export-led by 1988. Though even a sharp acceleration of US export growth coincided with a large current account deficit, it was sufficient to reduce the current account deficit from 3.6 per cent of GNP in 1987 to 2.6 per cent of GNP in 1988.

The distress of the traded goods sector in 1984–5, coupled with persistent large external deficits set in motion two forces. The first was heavy lobbying by American industry for a trade bill with emphasis on opening up foreign markets and the removal of non-tariff barriers said to be impeding sales abroad.

Second, at the Plaza meeting in September 1985 the Reagan Administration reversed its stance on the dollar and indicated a willingness and indeed a perceived need for dollar depreciation, expecting to see a subsequent, sharp reduction in the US external deficit. Rapid growth in the US money stock accompanied, temporarily, by monetary tightening in Japan, gave additional momentum to a dollar depreciation that had begun earlier in 1985.

The extreme pressure on international competitiveness of American manufacturing during the 1981–5 period resulted in structural adjustments that meant that the American current account balance would likely be less responsive to exchange rate adjustment than has historically been the case. As a result of a long-sustained real appreciation of the dollar, many American companies accelerated or initiated plans to locate manufacturing facilities abroad. Such relocation of manufacturing facilities and the implication it carries for a tendency to understate US exports is not likely to be reversed. These facilities will be maintained and perhaps expanded as a hedge against the problems of competing in world markets that flow from exchange rate volatility, that in turn results from a failure to co-ordinate economic policies among major industrial countries.

The internationalization of American business has of course been matched by internationalization of businesses whose managements are based in other countries. A typical pattern sees managerial expertise in financial and research areas headquartered in a home or base country with manufacturing facilities located around the world. This is partly due to the above-mentioned need to hedge against sharp changes in exchange rates. It is also likely to be due to the economies of scale that can be realized through centralized financial and managerial capital (see Makin, 1974). A multinational firm that operates world wide, sourcing and manufacturing in markets dictated by financial and real market conditions, is very likely to be an increasingly prevalent phenomenon. The rapidly increasing presence of 'American' firms in Europe and Japan and 'Japanese' and 'European' firms manufacturing and operating in the United States only serves to underscore this point.

There are many implications for policy-makers that flow from such internationalization of businesses. First, standard measures of merchandise trade balances may have to be discarded, or at least read with additional qualifications in mind. The more a country's firms tend to locate abroad their manufacturing facilities, the smaller will be that country's recorded commodity exports. Yet, such a weak showing on traditional merchandise trade figures may mask a sharp increase in dominance in world markets by the country's manufacturers.

The results of American budgetary and tax policy in the 1980s will also require a rethinking of policies developed largely in a closed economy setting. When investment incentive measures were enacted into the tax code in 1981, no thought was given by American policy-makers to the possibility that the budgetary implications of revenues lost through investment incentives, coupled with deficit increases resulting from other spending measures, would result in exchange-rate appreciation large enough to blunt the impact of tax incentives on investment. The crowding out of investment occurred *ex post* due to currency appreciation instead of *ex ante* due to higher interest rates. Unfortunately, the new investment could not be undone in the face of *ex post* crowding out. The new investments have since, given the depreciation of the dollar, become more viable, but the delayed positive returns were costly to await.

More broadly, the advisability of tax measures designed to

enhance competitiveness where exports are capital intensive is called into question by traditional trade theory. If a country like the United States enacts measures that lead to a large increase in the capital stock then, as we know from the Rybczynski theorem, the relative price of capital-intensive exports will fall or, equivalently, the United States' terms of trade will deteriorate. The result is that, to the extent that its exports are capital intensive, many of the supposed benefits of investment incentives spill out of the United States to the rest of the world.

3. Sustainability of the 1980s' International 'Imbalances'

The continued high level of capital inflows to the United States after the cessation of official pegging of the dollar following the market crash, has surprised some who argued that the growing 'net debtor' status of the United States would deter foreign investment. It appears either that the US net debtor status has been overblown (see Makin, 1988a) or that pressures outside of the United States for diversification of rapidly growing portfolios remain strong. It is true that aggregate portfolios outside the United States are now approximately twice the size of aggregate US portfolios. Further, foreign wealth is growing faster than American wealth. In 1988 these facts implied a net foreign demand for US assets equal to about $130 billion or 2.6 per cent of GNP.

These figures can be derived from a simple analysis of global saving. In 1987 gross national saving in the Big 5 (Japan, Germany, France, Canada, and Britain) totalled about $1412 billion versus $552 billion in the United States. The $1412 billion, over twice the US total, results from the fact that the combined size of the Big 5 is about twice that of the United States economy, and the elasticity, with respect to rising incomes, of demand for future goods is higher. US acquisition of foreign assets (private and official) totalled $76 billion in 1987, 13.8 per cent of national saving, while foreign acquisition of US assets was $211.5 billion or 15 per cent of national saving abroad. The difference, $135.5 billion, accounted for the bulk of the US $154 billion current account deficit in 1987. A parallel analysis rationalizes a 'sustainable' current account deficit of $135 billion for 1988.

The share of Big 5 gross saving being invested in the United States rose steadily from 1979 to 1986, while the share of US gross saving flowing abroad collapsed after 1982, largely as a result of the absorption by tax-enhanced investment opportunities (see Figure 3). After 1984 the share of US gross saving flowing abroad rose again as American companies sought to avoid strong dollar problems by relocating production and distribution facilities outside the United States. The real dollar exchange rate has moved with changes in the ratio of foreign acquisition of US assets to gross Big 5 saving.

There emerges from these data a picture of a rising share of foreign saving flowing to the United States after 1979. This followed from the pull of relatively high US real interest rates and the push of foreign deregulation. The process slowed after 1986, by which time foreign deregulation was largely complete and most new post-deregulation portfolio goals of Big 5 investors had been achieved. After 1987 normal investment flows from greatly enlarged foreign portfolios have created a sustainable net capital inflow to the United States of over $100 billion annually.

Accompanying these portfolio adjustments there emerged during 1988 an oscillatory pattern of exchange rates that followed developments in the US economy, policy, and merchandise trade balance. As a result of large wealth losses accompanying the stock market collapse of 1987, American absorption fell and personal saving rose by about $45 billion per year. The unexpected reduction in American absorption was reflected in lower current account and merchandise trade deficits. In turn, the unexpected reduction in the American external 'imbalance' caused foreign investors to renew purchases of dollar assets and produced some modest strengthening of the dollar at mid-year.

The Federal Reserve also contributed to a slowdown in the growth of American absorption by initiating a programme of monetary stringency in April 1988. The growth rate of monetary aggregates was slowed and interest rates were allowed to rise. At first the increase in the federal funds rate was steady but gradual, with a rise of about 150 basis points over the seven months between April and December 1988. Thereafter the rise in the federal funds rate accelerated with the next 150-basis point increase requiring less than three months. Meanwhile, the slowdown in the growth of all monetary aggregates continued.

It is likely that the environment of rapidly diversifying global portfolios outside the United States will, for a time at least, produce the unusual combination of an appreciating dollar and a falling merchandise trade deficit that reflects a slowing US economy. As US economic growth slows, American absorption of imports will be reduced, while American traded goods industries currently operating close to capacity will expand exports when domestic demand falls.

The resultant drop in the American merchandise trade deficit coupled with incipient pressure for capital inflows on the order of $120-130 billion per year will cause the dollar to appreciate to a point that equalizes desired capital inflows with the current-account deficit. If desired capital inflows rise to the $150-160 billion annual range, as apparently they have in 1989, heavy official sales of dollars will be required to prevent dollar appreciation. To the extent that such intervention is not allowed to affect relative money supplies, the large 'imbalances' decried by managed-traders will persist.

Of course a corollary of this outcome is the proposition that a large (greater than $100 billion per year) American current account deficit is sustainable. Contrary to the Feldstein (1988) and Bergsten *et al.* (1987) views that foreign investors will require stiffer and stiffer terms to continue net lending to the United States at a $100 billion-plus annual rate, a simple portfolio stock adjustment view coupled with the international perspective of portfolio managers points to an easily sustainable net $100 billion-plus capital inflow to the United States.

The major threats to such sustainability are inflationary US monetary policy or unilaterally imposed arbitrary restrictions on foreign investment in the United States, like those ominously lurking in the Bryant Amendment which has resurfaced after its elimination from the 1988 Trade Bill; but they can be controlled by the United States provided that the necessary will exists. The major new constraint on the United States as a net borrower (and net debtor in book-value if not market-value terms) is less freedom to risk inflation in the name of stimulating growth and less freedom to indulge in symbolic, xenophobic measures against foreign investors.

Having suggested that large persistent imbalances are 'sustainable' I do not wish to leave the impression that *any* level of imbalances over *any* length of time should be ignored. Undeniably, the American level of absorption during the 1980s has been unusually high. Expansionary fiscal policy, and an unusually low level of personal saving combined with growing investment flows have required capital inflows that were available on good terms. Obviously, continued growth of American absorption, financed by an ever-increasing flow of net foreign borrowing would, at the very least, result in growing concern about future American standards of living.

In fact, the large intertemporal swap between America and its trading partners is beginning to wind down. Figure 5 shows a reduction in US net foreign borrowing during 1988 that was due largely to a one percentage point rise in the personal saving rate from 3.2 per cent of disposable personal income in 1987 to 4.2 per cent in 1988 that represented a cut in absorption of about $45 billion. Wealth losses due to lower stock and bond prices and real dollar depreciation may have been partly responsible.

Early 1989 data suggest, so far, a continued rise in the personal saving rate. Another one percentage point increase back toward the long-run average personal-saving rate of about 6.5 per cent would reduce the 1989 US net external borrowing requirement by another $45 billion and the GNP share of net external borrowing to about 1.6 per cent. A personal saving rate at the long run average of 6.5 per cent would virtually eliminate the American net external borrowing requirement.

American tax measures to encourage saving would be the best way to reduce persistent external 'imbalances' and thereby to discourage protectionist policies. Taxing half of interest income while allowing deduction of only half of interest expense would help to eliminate the current tax code bias in favour of borrowing and spending, and against saving and lending. It would also produce a net revenue gain and an attendant reduction in American net borrowing needs. Since much of interest income now accrues to pension funds and is already tax exempt, the revenue loss from taxing only half of interest income would be less than the revenue gain from allowing deduction of only half of interest expense.

4. Concluding Remarks

The primary danger emanating from the perception that large international 'imbalances' exist is not that they will one day become unsustainable. Rather it is that global portfolio growth and

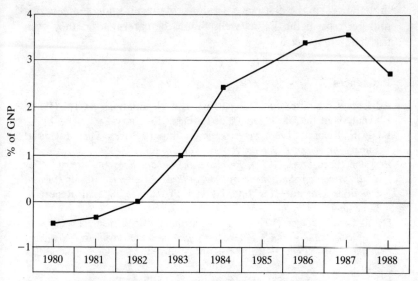

Figure 5.   US net foreign borrowing as a share of GNP.
Source: Bureau of Economic Analysis, US Dept. of Commerce.

diversification will make such 'imbalances' too sustainable and their persistence, contrary to conventional expectations, will result in calls for unilateral measures to reduce 'imbalances' that are seen, largely without foundation, as the result of 'unfair' trade practices.

Such calls are already being heard in the United States. Once the false notion that bilateral balance ought to be the outcome of 'fair' trade was embedded in the 1988 US Trade Bill, the stage was set for considerable mischief.

Once one accepts the notion that a persistent bilateral 'imbalance' is, *de facto*, evidence of unfair trade practices, there is a sharp rise in the likelihood of recommendations for export or import quotas or other protectionist measures if the goals of 'results-oriented' trade policy are not met.

A great irony that might arise from the large, multilateral, international 'imbalances' of the 1980s would see unilateral American efforts to extinguish bilateral 'imbalances' resulting in a reversal of the post-war trend towards trade liberalization and, ultimately, in unsustainability of the multilateral 'imbalances' that created the ill-advised 'results-oriented' approach to bilateral 'imbalances' in the first place. In short, managed traders in America and perhaps in the EC as well, should be careful what they wish for. They may get it.

References

Advisory Committee for Trade Policy and Negotiations ACTN (1989), 'Analysis of the US–Japan Trade Problem' February.

Baldwin, Richard (1988), 'Hysteresis on Import Prices: The Beachhead Effect', *American Economic Review*, vol. 78, pp. 773–85.

Bergsten, Fred *et al.* (1987), *Resolving the Global Economic Crisis: After Wall Street*, A Statement by Thirty-three Economists from Thirteen Countries (Institute for International Economics, Special Report 6, December).

Dornbusch, Rudiger (1988), 'The Adjustment Mechanism: Theory and Problems', in Norman S. Feleke (ed.), *International Payments Imbalances in the 1980s* (Federal Reserve Bank of Boston, Conference Series no 32).

Feldstein, Martin (1988), 'Feldstein on the Dollar', *The Economist* (December 3), pp. 21–4.

Frankel, Jeffrey A. (1985), 'Six Possible Meanings of "Overvaluation": The 1981–85 Dollar' (Princeton Essays in International Finance, no. 159, December).

Fukao, Mitsukiro and Kunio Okina (1988), 'Internationalization of Financial Markets and Balance of Payments Imbalances: A Japanese Perspective' (Institute of Monetary and Economic Studies, The Bank of Japan, July).

Hooper, Peter and C. L. Mann (1989) 'The Emergence and Persistence of the US External Imbalance: 1980–87' (Princeton Studies in International Finance, no. 65, October).

Kissinger, Henry and Cyrus Vance (1988), 'Bipartisan Objectives for Foreign Policy', *Foreign Affairs* (Summer), pp. 891–921.

Koo, Richard (1987), 'Japan and International Capital Flows' (Nomura Research Institute, Tokyo, October).

Krugman, Paul R. (1988) 'Long-Run Effects of the Strong Dollar', in R. Marston (ed.), *Misalignment of Exchange Rates: Effects on Trade and Industry* (Chicago: University of Chicago Press).

Makin, John H. (1974), 'Capital Flows and Exchange Rate Flexibility in the Post-Bretton Woods Era', *Essays in International Finance* (International Finance Section, Princeton University, February).

—— (1986), *US Fiscal Policy: Its Effects at Home and Abroad* (American Enterprise Institute, Washington DC).

—— (1988), 'The Impact of Fiscal Policy on the Balance of Payments:

Recent Experience in the United States' (American Enterprise Institute, Working Paper, no. 13, February).

Makin, John H. (1988*a*), 'The US "Debtor" Status Has Been Overblown', *The International Economy* (January / February), pp. 120–4.

—— (1988*b*), 'Japan's Threat', *Challenge* (November / December), pp. 8–16.

—— (1989), Statement before Committee on Ways and Means on the *National Saving Rate of the United States and its Trading Partners* (April 19).

Marris, Stephen (1985), *Deficits and the Dollar: The World Economy at Risk* (Institute for International Economics, Washington, DC, December, revd. March 1986).

Prestowitz, Clyde (1988) *Trading Places: How We Allowed Japan to Take The Lead* (New York: Basic Books).

Sachs, Jeffrey D. (1988), 'Global Adjustments to a Shrinking US Trade Deficit', *Brookings Papers on Economic Activity* 2, pp. 639–68.

US External Debt and Systemic Implications for the Dollar

SECOND PRIZE

Editors' Introduction

This essay by Giorgio Gomel of the Banca d'Italia, winner of the Second Prize, deals with the issue of the sustainability of the now large external debt of the USA and the corresponding large debt-servicing requirement. Whether it can be sustained depends on both its size relative to the US economy, and whether foreigners are prepared to continue to hold greater and greater amounts of US debt. This may have important implications for the continued position of the dollar as the world's key currency.

In terms of sovereign risk the author argues that the US economy can sustain a further build-up in external debt as long as the current account deficit declines relative to GNP. The 'peculiarity' of the US case is that it borrows internationally in its own currency so that its external debts consist of dollar claims held by non-residents who fully incur exchange rate risk. It will be then the unwillingness of lenders to incur further US dollar risk, rather than their assessment of the US credit-worthiness as a sovereign borrower, which might undermine its ability to finance its external deficit. The author concludes that over the medium term private holdings of dollars will have to rise, which will only be feasible at a lower dollar exchange rate or if US interest rates rise.

The outlook for the role of the dollar as the key currency is uncertain. While international transactions are still dominated by the dollar, the fluctuation of its exchange rate might force investors to look to other currencies.

Giorgio Gomel, 40, is the Chief of the International Economics Division of the Bank of Italy's Research Department. He was educated at the University of Torino and Columbia University, New York, where he was a Fulbright Scholar and received his M.Phil. in economics. He has taught at Columbia, Fairleigh Dickinson University, the University of Cosenza, and John Cabot College in Rome. In 1982–4 he was assistant to the Executive Director for Italy at the IMF. In 1988 he was a Visiting Fellow at Princeton University. His fields of interest include international policy co-ordination and European monetary and economic integration.

2

US External Debt and Systemic Implications for the Dollar

GIORGIO GOMEL*

'. . . the rich man's effect: people seem happy to lend to the
rich without asking too many questions.'
(A. Gutowski, 'Where is the dollar going?', as quoted by S.
Marris (1985))
'For one of the richest countries of the world it seems hardly
appropriate either to borrow currently on a massive scale
from the rest of the world or to be a net debtor before it.'
(H. Wallich, Statement before the Finance Committee, US
Senate, 23 March, 1984)

1. The United States as a Debtor Country: conceptual and definitional issues. The basic stylized facts

Table 1 reports the official figures on US external assets and liabilities, both as aggregates and in disaggregated form, broken down by main categories: (i) direct investment; (ii) corporate equity investment; (iii) debt instruments. This decomposition underscores the importance of distinguishing between three pertinent concepts: net international investment position (NIIP), net debt, and gross debt. The distinction is essential for the purpose of both interpreting correctly the basic facts and figures and making internationally consistent comparisons.

Most discussions of US external debt are based on the official NIIP measures, as computed and published yearly by the US Department of Commerce in the Survey of Current Business. A slightly aggregated and simplified version is presented in Table 2;

*The views expressed are the author's alone and do not represent those of the Banca d'Italia. The paper is based on research conducted during the Fall semester 1988 spent as Visiting Fellow at the Department of Economics, Princeton University. Comments and suggestions by Peter Kenen, Benjamin Friedman, Francesco Papadia, are gratefully acknowledged.

we intend to adopt a similar approach, although some distinctions and conceptual clarifications are in order.

The NIIP is defined as the difference between the country's claims on foreigners (assets) and foreign claims on it (liabilities) (see Table 1: All Investment, Net). *Gross debt* is the sum total of the country's foreign liabilities held in the form of debt instruments. The figures for gross debt are shown in the penultimate column of the table (debt instruments, liabilities). Lastly, *net debt* can be defined as gross debt minus all claims on foreigners held in the form of debt instruments.[1]

The NIIP as calculated by the Department of Commerce significantly differs from the net debt concept proposed above: it includes US official gold holdings as a component of US foreign assets (valued at an official price of $42 per ounce—we shall return to this point later), and direct investment or holdings of equity. Gold is a part of the country's net wealth but obviously not a liability or debt of a foreign country. Similarly, direct investment or equity acquisitions do not represent US liabilities nor do they entail future debt-service obligations on the part of US residents and vice versa.

Should we adopt the conventional definition of net (financial) debt, i.e. by subtracting direct and corporate equity investment from external assets and liabilities, the recorded history of the USA as a debtor would look significantly different. According to this yardstick, the United States became a net debtor in 1971 and continued to be so throughout the 1970s, restoring its net creditor position as recently as 1980 before becoming a debtor country again in 1985. Loosely speaking, the USA for a number of years had a net creditor position on direct investment and simultaneously a net financial debtor position. It was the sizeable and growing position in foreign direct investment, offsetting the debtor position in financial instruments, that made the United States a net creditor in the 1970s (in terms of NIIP, see column 1 in Table 1). The net direct investment position began to deteriorate after 1980 and quite rapidly so in subsequent years, largely because of growing foreign direct investment in the USA while US investment overseas remained fairly stable; the USA became a net debtor on direct investment in 1988. Moreover, foreign holdings of corporate equity in the USA increased rapidly while US portfolio acquisitions of foreign equities fluctuated around a slightly upward trend; by 1984

Table 1 US international investment position (US$ billions, year-end)

Year	All Investment*			Direct Investment*			Corporate Equity			Debt Instruments		
	Assets	Liabilities	Net†	Assets	Liabilities	Net†	Assets	Liabilities	Net†	Assets	Liabilities	Net†
1970:	165	107	58	75	13	62	7	27	−21	72	66	6
1975:	295	221	74	124	28	96	10	36	−26	150	158	−8
1980:	607	501	106	215	83	132	19	65	−45	361	353	8
1981:	720	579	141	228	109	120	18	64	−46	463	406	57
1982:	825	688	137	208	125	83	19	76	−57	587	487	100
1983:	874	784	90	207	137	70	26	96	−70	630	551	79
1984:	896	892	4	211	165	46	27	95	−68	647	632	15
1985:	950	1061	−111	230	185	45	40	124	−84	680	751	−71
1986:	1073	1341	−268	260	220	40	50	167	−117	763	954	−191
1987:	1170	1548	−378	308	272	36	55	173	−118	807	1103	−296
1988:	1254	1786	−532	327	329	−2	63	198	−135	864	1259	−395

Notes:

* Official gold holdings are included in total assets.

† Not always exactly equal to the difference between assets and liabilities due to rounding.

Source: US Dept. of Commerce, *Survey of Current Business.*

Table 2 US international investment position, selected years, 1970–87 (US$ billions)

	1970	1975	1980	1981	1982	1983	1984	1985	1986	1987	1988
NET POSITION:											
Net Creditor (+) or Debtor (−)	58.5	74.2	106.3	141.1	137.0	89.6	3.6	−110.7	−267.8	−378.3	−532.5
TOTAL ASSETS (US Investment Abroad):	165.4	295.1	607.1	719.8	824.9	873.9	896.1	950.3	1,073.3	1,169.7	1,253.6
US Government	46.6	58.0	90.5	98.8	108.5	113.3	119.8	130.8	138.0	134.2	133.3
Private	118.8	237.1	516.6	621.1	716.4	760.7	776.3	819.5	935.2	1,035.4	1,120.4
Direct Investment	75.5	124.0	215.4	228.3	207.8	207.2	211.5	230.3	259.8	308.0	326.9
Portfolio Investment	20.9	34.9	62.7	63.4	75.5	83.8	89.1	112.8	131.7	146.7	156.8
US Claims on Unaffiliated Foreigners Reported by US Non-Banks	8.5	18.3	34.7	35.9	28.6	35.1	30.1	29.1	36.4	31.2	32.9
US Claims Reported by US Banks	13.8	59.8	203.9	293.5	404.6	434.5	445.6	447.3	507.3	549.4	603.8
TOTAL LIABILITIES (Foreign Investment in US):	106.9	220.9	500.8	578.7	688.0	784.3	892.5	1,061.0	1,341.1	1,548.0	1,786.2
Foreign Off. Assets in US	26.2	86.9	176.1	180.4	189.1	194.5	199.2	202.6	241.9	283.6	322.1
Private	80.8	134.0	324.8	398.3	498.9	589.8	693.3	858.4	1,099.1	1,264.4	1,464.1
Direct Investment	13.3	27.7	83.0	108.7	124.7	137.1	164.6	184.6	220.4	271.8	328.8
US Treasury Securities	1.2	4.2	16.1	18.5	25.8	33.8	58.2	83.6	91.4	78.4	96.6
Other Securities	34.8	45.7	74.1	75.1	93.0	113.7	127.3	206.3	308.8	344.3	393.6
US Liabilities to Unaffiliated Foreigners Reported by US Non-Banks	8.8	13.9	30.4	30.6	27.5	26.9	31.0	29.4	26.9	29.4	35.5
US Liabilities Reported by US Banks	22.7	42.5	121.1[1]	165.4	228.0	278.3	312.2	354.5	451.6	540.6	609.5

Note: Details may not add to totals due to rounding.   *Source:* US Dept. of Commerce, *Survey of Current Business.*

Table 3 The current account and net international investment position (NIIP) (US$ billions)

	1980	1981	1982	1983	1984	1985	1986	1987	1988
1. NIIP	016.3	141.1	137.0	89.6	3.6	−110.7	−267.8	−378.3	−532.5
2. Changes in NIIP	11.9	34.8	−4.1	−47.4	−86.0	−107.1	−157.1	−110.5	−154.2
3. Current Account	1.5	8.1	−7.0	−44.3	−104.2	−112.7	−133.2	−143.7	−126.5
4. Statistical discrepancy	25.0	18.7	34.4	9.1	23.9	15.3	11.3	1.9	−10.6
5. Adjusted NIIP	43.4	59.5	21.0	−35.5	−145.4	−275.0	−443.4	−555.8	−699.4

Note: The adjusted position (line 5) is computed by subtracting the statistical discrepancy (line 4) from the recorded position (line 1) on a cumulative basis beginning in 1978. It is assumed that the statistical discrepancy represents unrecorded capital inflows into the USA.

Source: Own calculations on US Dept. of Commerce data.

the combined net position in direct investment and corporate equity holdings (columns 2 and 3, Table 1) had turned negative.

No matter what preferred standard of measurement is adopted (NIIP or net debt), the important fact concerning US external debt is not its size, but the speed of its buildup in recent years. This has reflected rapidly widening current account deficits which have been financed essentially by the net accumulation of dollar-denominated claims by the rest of the world.

This stock-flow interaction is represented in Figure 1. The net investment position changed little as a percentage of GNP during most of the 1970s, reaching a peak in 1975, equalled afterwards in 1982; thereafter it declined sharply, turning significantly negative in 1985, as was earlier recalled.[2] Between 1981, when the net position reached its peak (plus $141 billion) and 1985, the current account deteriorated by $124 billion, largely because of the growing trade deficit (the other components—net investment income, other services, unrequited transfers—contributed a further $30 billion to that out-turn). As a consequence the NIIP suffered a negative shift of $250 billion.

Figure 2 illustrates the diverging dynamics of US external assets and liabilities; the deterioration in the net position resulted from the acceleration of foreign-owned assets in the USA which outpaced the growth of US claims on foreigners by over 10 per cent annually during the first half of the 1980s.[3]

As a consequence of the recent rapid increase of foreign-owned assets in the USA, investment income payments (loosely speaking, the 'external debt service') have considerably increased. Of the major statistically identified components of investment income— earnings from direct investment, other (financial) private investment, US government—only the first continues to show large net receipts owing to the fact that US direct investment overseas is larger than foreign investment in the USA. Payments to foreigners on US government securities have consistently outpaced receipts from US government-owned foreign assets over the last several years. Finally, payments to foreigners on other (financial) private investments have, in contrast, grown prominently in recent years, owing to the expansion of foreign-owned private assets in the USA and relatively high US interest rates, exceeding receipts for the first time in 1987.

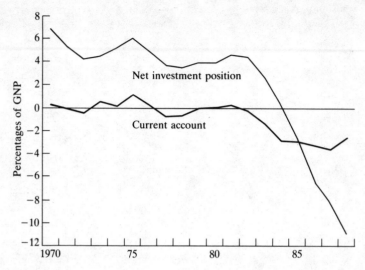

Figure 1. US current account and net international investment position (% of GNP)
Source: US Dept. of Commerce, *Survey of Current Business.*

2. Some Measurement Problems. Implications of adjusting the recorded international investment position

It is commonly recognized that the recorded NIIP as presented in the preceding section suffers from a multitude of measurement and valuation problems.

The need for correcting at least some of the implied distortions in the data, the method proposed for this purpose, and the implications for the present analysis will be briefly discussed in this section.

The statistical discrepancy (see line 4 in Table 3) has become a prominent item in US balance-of-payments figures since the late 1970s. According to most analysts, including the official compilers of the statistics (Department of Commerce), the discrepancy is largely accounted for by unrecorded capital inflows into the United States. It follows that the recorded data understate US external liabilities and hence overstate the net external position. A rough calculation, based on the simplifying assumption that the discrepancy reflects only unrecorded capital flows towards the USA,[4]

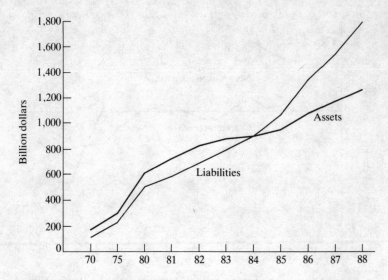

Figure 2. US external assets and liabilities: selected years (US% billions)
Source: US Dept. of Commerce, *Survey of Current Business*.

would indicate that the USA became a net debtor as early as 1983, rather than in 1985: its negative position would be in the neighbourhood of $700 billion. This correction alone, however, would grossly and erroneously overstate America's debtor status.

Two other issues should be mentioned. First, direct investment is measured at book value, hence significantly underestimated; the distortion is greater for US investment overseas which is larger and 'older', entailing a potentially wider divergence between book and market values. On this account US external assets are evidently understated.

On a second matter, it has been argued by some that official gold holdings which are valued at $42 per ounce should be recorded at market prices, thus reducing the net debtor position by a significant amount. We have stated, however, against this line of reasoning, that US gold holdings are no one's debt and should therefore be excluded from the estimation of the NIIP. Notwithstanding the measurement errors, a perusal of the time series in Tables 1, 2 and 3 consistently indicate that both the aggregated NIIP and its broad components (direct investment, corporate equity, and debt investments) have rapidly worsened in recent years.

As was suggested in the preceding section, the precise magnitude of the US external position is not so important for analytical purposes as the dynamics of the US transition from creditor to debtor status and the speed of accumulation of further debt.

> 'The stability of our capital and money markets is now dependent as never before on the willingness of foreigners to continue to place growing amounts of money in our markets.'
> (P. Volcker, Statement before Senate Committee, 20 February 1985)

3. The problem of Sustainability

3.1. Introduction and basic definitions

No single, universally accepted, method is available for addressing the question of whether the United States' external debt and deficit are sustainable in the sense that they can be financed at the currently prevailing exchange and interest rates.

In discussing the meaning and operational content of sustainability, we can roughly categorize it into three types.

First, sustainability can be assessed in a *flow* sense: the US current-account deficit or capital inflows implied by the prevailing level of interest rates and of the dollar (even after its sizeable depreciation from peak values) may be larger than feasible. Specifically, it may be difficult to attract capital inflows at the rates necessary to sustain the dollar at roughly its present level (at current interest rates) in the face of current-account deficits exceeding $100 billion over the medium term.[5]

Second, there is a *stock* view: the net accumulation of dollar-denominated assets by the rest of the world may result in too large a share of net claims on the USA in the total net financial holdings of non-residents. In other words, US external indebtedness may be 'too much' given the current constellation of yields on dollar assets relative to assets denominated in competing currencies.[6]

Third, the issue of sustainability has a multi-faceted political dimension. Besides the conventional arguments of the possible resurgence of protectionist sentiment in the USA[7] and loss of status or primacy in the balance of international economic power, two other considerations are worth mentioning here. One is the possibility that foreign countries may decide to restrict capital exports to the USA, out of concern for the diversion of savings away from domestic investment or because of growing apprehension about protectionist responses elicited in the USA by the persistence of external deficits. The second is the possibility that the USA will itself act to limit foreign capital inflows because of the feared loss of economic and political independence.[8]

We will focus in the remainder of this section on sustainability in a *stock* sense.

3.2. Sustainability: the very long run

The question of 'too much' external debt or of the limits to its accumulation was addressed in the mid-eighties by Islam (1984), Marris (1985), and Krugman (1985), among others. Both simple projections and model simulations supported the view that the capital inflows needed to sustain the dollar at roughly its 1985 level would raise US external debt to unsustainable magnitudes by the 1990s.

The question can still be asked today whether, over a long-term horizon, foreigners holding claims on the USA might perceive them as too large relative to the country's ability to service its debt, and, in such a case, whether this would precipitate a debt or currency crisis such as to jeopardize the servicing of US external liabilities or the status of the dollar as key international currency. The issue can be addressed by assessing conventional credit-worthiness indicators and comparing the USA with the situation of other major debtor nations, both developing and industrial.[9]

For this purpose, we draw on a set of calculations prepared by the OECD; these are based on an extrapolation of medium-term projections (from 1988 to 1992).[10] Under some reasonable macro-economic assumptions,[11] the key debt indicators would look like the following:

Under these projections, the debt-to-GNP ratio would reach 17 per cent in 1994 and rise to over 18 per cent by the year 2000.[12] The debt-to-exports ratio would peak in the 1990s, and decline slowly thereafter. Net interest payments could exceed 10 per cent of the total value of exports of goods and non-factor services.

The net flow of interest payments on the accumulated debt could amount to $116 billion annually by the year 2000; hence, given the working hypothesis of a $100 billion current account deficit each

Table 4 US debt indicators (% ratios)

	1987	1994	2000
Net international position (NIIP)/GNP	−8.2	−17.1	−18.3
Net international position (NIIP)/Exports	−114.0	−168.8	−161.3
Net investment income/GNP	0.3	−1.1	−1.2
Net investment income/Exports	4.5	−10.6	−10.6

year,[13] US trade in goods and non-factor services ought to generate a small surplus by the end of the projection period.

This can be seen in a slightly different fashion. Let us define B as the non-interest current account measured as a fraction of GNP. Let r be the real interest rate and g the growth rate of the US economy. Then the growth of the debt-to-GNP ratio (D) will be $dD/dt = -B + (r-g)D$.

To keep debt from rising faster than GNP, there needs to be a current surplus (or real resource transfer) equal to $(r-g)$ times the value of the debt.

The projected values of credit-worthiness indicators of Table 4 do not compare unfavourably with the current experience of a number of heavily indebted industrial nations. For instance, in terms of debt-to-GNP ratios, Canada, Sweden, Australia, Denmark, and others record much higher ratios than those calculated for the USA for the year 2000. Similarly, the debt service ratio (net interest payments as a fraction of exports) for these countries exceeds the peak value for the USA.

As a tentative conclusion of this discussion we suggest that the projected future path of US foreign debt is not unsustainable in the long run. In the scenario postulated in Table 4 the cost of servicing the debt will remain just slightly above 1 per cent of GNP assuming that the negative investment position reaches $1.7 trillion. This outcome will entail an adverse shift (or real resource transfer abroad) of only 1.5 per cent of GNP over a time-span of more than ten years (between 1987 and the year 2000).

If such a shift is not financed through additional external borrowing but accommodated through increased net exports of goods and non-factor services, real spending growth in the USA will have to decelerate. Domestic absorption will have to grow at rates below those of domestic income in order to correct the over-absorption (equal to the current-account deficit) which has ranged around 3 per cent of nominal GNP in the past 4 years.

Questions can be raised as to the analytical and operational relevance of conventional debt indicators and international comparisons based on them. Two points are important: (i) sovereign-risk considerations are largely irrelevant for the USA; and (ii) exchange risk arising from the currency denomination of US foreign debt can become a significant constraint.

On the first point, it can be noted that US foreign debt largely consists of dollar-denominated debt instruments held by non-residents. These instruments are mostly negotiated and exchanged between foreigners and residents on the US market without ever 'leaving' this market; changes in the net external position of the USA thus reflect shifts in the composition of claims between foreign and domestic portfolio holders. It is, therefore, crucial to distinguish between sovereign risk and currency risk.

The distinctive feature of the US situation is that external financing takes the form of net acquisition of dollar claims by the rest of the world because of the dominant position of the dollar as an international currency (see section 4 below). This is in obvious contrast with the experience of other debtor countries whose external liabilities are generally denominated in the currencies of the lenders or in third currencies.

It follows that, although the USA will not experience an LDC-style debt crisis, a currency crisis is a possible occurrence.[14] Given the dollar denomination of US debt, foreigners bear the exchange rate risk. Thus, there may be limits on US external indebtedness which are likely to be determined more by foreign investors' willingness to incur exchange risk as their exposure in dollars increases than by their assessment of US credit-worthiness as a sovereign borrower.

3.3. Sustainability: the short run

No definitive conclusion can be drawn about the sustainable long-run path of US foreign debt from the projections of debt indicators. The future profile of current account deficits is crucial in determining the path of debt. As was suggested at the end of the previous section, the issue of sustainability may, however,

Table 5 Holdings of dollar-denominated assets by private foreigners (stocks, in US$ billions)

	1985	1986	1987
1. US Treasury securities	84	91	78
2. Other US securities	206	308	344
3. Other US non-bank liabilities	29	26	29
4. Non-bank deposits with US banks	74	81	81
TOTAL in USA	309	415	454
5. Eurocurrency liabilities to non-banks	199	223	241
6. Eurodollar and foreign (dollar) bonds	237	293	320
GRAND TOTAL	745	931	1015

Note: Total includes both assets issued by the USA and held by foreigners and dollar assets issued and held by foreigners; it excludes interbank positions.

Sources: for lines 1, 2, 3 Survey of Current Business; for line 4, IMF, International Financial Statistics; for line 5, BIS, International Banking and Financial Market Developments, table 3B (reporting banks' external positions in dollars vis-à-vis nonbanks); for line 6, BIS, ibidem, table 8 (Euro and foreign bonds in dollars): it is assumed that one-quarter of bonds is held by US residents, therefore to be excluded.

become relevant over a much shorter time horizon, if foreigners are not prepared to absorb increasing proportions of dollar-denominated assets into their portfolios as implied by continuing US current account deficits. Growing exposure to exchange risk by private dollar asset holders may thus require continuing increases in the expected relative yield of dollar assets, either via a widening of interest rate differentials or a depreciating dollar.

In this section we provide some rough and tentative estimates of foreigners' holdings of dollar-denominated assets, discuss the constraints arising from such composition of international portfolios in the present situation, and explore some likely implications for the future course of the dollar.

One point must be underlined at the outset of the analysis. It relates to the need to distinguish between claims on the USA and claims denominated in dollars. Because of the dollar's status as the dominant international currency, there exists a stock of

Table 6 Holdings of dollar-denominated assets by private
foreigners (percentage ratios of GNP in OECD
countries, excluding the USA)

	1975	1980	1984	1985	1986	1987
Grand total (from Table 7)						
At current prices and exchange rates	5	8	18	15.5	14.2	12.7
At current prices and 1980 exchange rates	5	8	11	9.2	10.5	10.5

Sources: from 1975 to 1984, Marris (1985); for later years, own
calculations.

dollar-denominated assets (generated by the Eurodollar and Eurobond markets) which do not represent claims on the USA but on other countries that have issued dollar liabilities. But the behaviour of the dollar exchange and interest rates depends on portfolio shifts of dollar assets, and not just US assets, in international markets. A conventional 'portfolio' approach, positing a close correspondence between shifts in the US current account and the proportion of US liabilities in foreign portfolios, would therefore be inadequate for the purpose of the present analysis. Despite data limitations, we will assess the outlook based on best available estimates of stocks and flows of dollar assets held by public and private non-US residents.

The decomposition of dollar holdings between the private and the public sector may be in part inaccurate since central banks of some developing countries often behave in ways similar to private portfolio holders; the same applies to state and local governments or public enterprises. But the distinction will be retained here in assessing the outlook for sustainability.

Following Marris (1985), we first estimate the size of the foreign (non-bank) portfolio of dollar-denominated assets. The major items are described in Table 5.

The total figure of around $1 trillion at end-1987 is the private (stock) demand for dollar assets. In Table 6 we measure this 'world portfolio' as a ratio to GNP in the OECD countries minus the USA (as a rough approximation of the rest of the world). This ratio was 5 per cent in 1975, then surged to 8 in 1980 and sharply increased to 18 in 1984 as the dollar appreciated. With the subsequent decline of the American currency, the dollar share dropped eventually to 12.7 per cent in 1987. Adjusting for valuation effects, the increase between 1975 and 1984 was slower, reaching 11 per cent by the end of the period. It appears to have stabilized since at slightly above 10 per cent.

Another way of looking at the issue of sustainability is to estimate flow supplies of and demands for dollar holdings by non-residents— a procedure proposed by the OECD (see Table 7). The distinction between the private and the public sector's net dollar positions is important for the discussion of private versus official financing of the US current deficit in the recent experience and in the near-term outlook.

The world private sector's net holdings of dollar assets soared from 1978 onward. Until 1982 this upward trend was chiefly linked to (dollar) borrowing by the public sector outside the USA (see Table 7, line 5); there was no net supply of dollars from US current account deficits.[15] Since 1984 non-US public sector borrowing dropped sharply and the rapidly rising acquisitions of dollar assets by the non-US private sector began to be the counterpart of widening US current deficits. These net additions to non-US private portfolios though close to $100 billion in both 1985 and 1986 ran below US current deficits as non-G10 and (in 1986) G10 countries increased official dollar reserves.

A dramatic shift occurred in 1987 when net private absorption of dollar assets was almost nil and the large US deficit was financed (nearly $140 billion) by an increase in dollar holdings by foreign monetary authorities (including a $9 billion reduction in US official reserves).[16] Official financing had been a much smaller fraction in earlier years (37 per cent in 1986 and roughly 8 per cent in 1984 and 1985).

Net private capital inflows into the USA recovered in 1988; in particular, portfolio investment picked up as exchange-rate expectations stabilized and interest-rate differentials moved increasingly in favour of dollar holdings. A tentative appraisal of events in 1988 suggests that foreign private investors' dollar exposure has not reached a critical value of saturation; thus the dramatic slow-down in net dollar accumulation in 1987 might be seen as a 'pause' along a trend, rather than a break in portfolio

Table 7 Dollar asset supply and demand (flows, US$ billions)

	1975	1980	1983	1984	1985	1986	1987
Supply:							
1. US current-account deficits	-18.1	-1.9	46.3	107.0	116.4	141.4	154.0
2. US official capital outflows	2.0	4.6	4.0	4.9	2.0	0.2	2.0
3. US direct investment abroad (net)	11.6	2.3	-11.6	-22.6	-1.0	3.0	-2.4
4. Balance on US non-financial transactions*	-4.5	5.0	38.7	89.3	116.6	144.6	153.6
5. Borrowing by non-US official sector†	13.6	21.3	11.4	-8.4	-8.0	2.0	-11.0
6. Total supply‡	9.1	26.3	50.1	80.9	108.6	146.6	142.6
Demand:							
7. Dollar reserves of non-G10 countries¶	-3.7	-0.1	5.0	13.2	9.2	8.9	45.0
8. Dollar reserves of G10 countries§	0.1	-9.1	0.6	-4.4	-0.1	43.2	94.1
9. Residual: absorption of dollar assets by non-US private sector**	12.7	35.5	44.5	72.1	99.5	94.5	3.5

Notes: * Line 1 plus line 2 plus line 3. † This item is referred to as 'compensatory finance', i.e. dollar borrowing by the public sector outside the USA. Net flows (+ sign = increase). ‡ Line 4 plus line 5. ¶ Changes (+ sign = increase). § Figures include the USA. Total is sum of increase in official dollar holdings, uses of US official reserve assets and issues of 'Carter bonds'. ** Line 6 minus lines 7 and 8.

asset composition. With the dollar depreciation, total holdings of dollar-denominated assets by private foreigners as a percentage of GNP declined in 1987 (see Table 6). Since exposure to exchange risk was somewhat reduced and exchange-rate expectations appeared to stabilize, there was room for stronger dollar absorption by the private sector in 1988.

Concerning the medium-term outlook, one can conjecture that if foreign investors were satisfied with the share of dollar assets in their portfolios at end-1987 and if world portfolios were growing at, say, 10 per cent a year in nominal terms, then a net demand of the order of $100 billion per year would emerge, enough to finance prospective US current deficits of roughly that magnitude.

But, according to most medium-term forecasts, US deficits will continue to exceed that amount. Thus, barring sustained official intervention on a scale such as in 1987,[17] the dollar share in private portfolios would have to rise, requiring a lower dollar or higher US interest rates.

At some point, foreign lenders may insist on denominating new claims on the US in currencies other than the dollar or may switch the currency denomination of their existing assets away from the dollar, thus shifting the exchange risk on US borrowers. There has already been a significant shift toward borrowing in foreign currencies. Bond issues denominated in foreign currencies placed directly abroad by US corporations rose from $800 million in 1984 to $10.5 billion in 1986, though falling to $4 billion in 1987. If this process were to continue on a sustained basis, it would have sizeable effects on the dollar's status as an international currency.

4. The Dollar as the Dominant International Currency: the systemic implications of the US debtor status

In this section we will explore the status of the dollar as international currency and point out diversification in the currency denomination of both official reserves and private investors' portfolios. We will distinguish this from the 'vehicle-currency' function of the dollar in foreign-exchange trading. The relevant empirical data will be reviewed. We will then discuss—in a rudimentary fashion, rather conjectural in nature—the question whether the dollar's dominance can be preserved when it is backed by an economy which continues to accumulate foreign debt.

4.4. The international position of the dollar: some basic magnitudes

We present some quantitative evidence on the current status of the dollar, distinguishing its functions as means of payment in foreign-exchange trading, official reserve asset, and store of value in international financial markets.

(*i*) *Means of payment* The dollar is still the chief currency in foreign-exchange trading and performs a significant 'third currency' role in transactions in which no US resident is involved. No precise statistical evidence is available to indicate whether this role of the dollar has altered significantly in recent years, but anecdotal evidence suggests that no major changes have occurred.

(*ii*) *Reserve asset* In his 1983 study, Peter Kenen reported that the developing countries were first in embarking on currency diversification: the share of the dollar fell sharply from almost 73 per cent at end-1976 to a low of about 60 at end-1980; the developed countries' share did not begin to fall until 1978 and the fall was not dramatic. According to central bankers surveyed by the Group of Thirty, 'diversification started when the dollar weakened on the foreign-exchange markets, but it was perpetuated by other motives, including the increase of uncertainty with the advent of floating exchange rates'. 'Changes in the use of the dollar in international trade and financial markets', states Kenen, 'are more readily explained by the increase in uncertainty resulting from the change in the exchange rate regime than by fluctuations in actual exchange rates.'[18]

A not-too-different appraisal is suggested by recent changes in the currency composition of foreign exchange reserves.[19] The dollar share increased slightly for all countries combined from 1980 to 1984, largely reflecting the dollar appreciation; adjusting for exchange-rate changes, it was almost unchanged. It declined in 1985 to 64.2 per cent, then rose in 1986 to 66 per cent and again in 1987 to 67 per cent. The 1987 increase, of considerable amount even after the valuation adjustment, resulted mainly from industrial countries' central bank intervention in support of the dollar (Table 8). For the developing countries, diversification appears stronger and more sustained, as in previous periods of protracted dollar weakness. The dollar share declined from almost 65 per cent in

Table 8 Share of national currencies in total identified official holdings of foreign exchange, end of year* (%)

	1975	1980	1984	1985	1986	1987	Memorandum: ECUs treated separately† 1987
All countries							
US dollar	79.4	68.6	69.4	64.2	66.0	67.1	56.9
Pound sterling	3.9	2.9	3.0	3.1	2.8	2.6	2.4
Deutschemark	6.3	14.9	12.3	14.9	14.9	14.7	13.6
French franc	0.8	1.7	1.1	1.3	1.2	1.2	1.1
Swiss franc	1.6	3.2	2.1	2.3	1.9	1.6	1.6
Netherlands guilder	1.0	1.3	0.8	1.0	1.1	1.1	1.1
Japanese yen	0.5	4.3	5.7	7.8	7.6	7.0	6.4
Unspecified currencies	6.5	3.1	5.8	5.4	4.5	4.7	16.9
Industrial countries							
US dollar	87.3	77.6	73.6	65.4	68.4	70.6	55.7
Pound sterling	1.1	0.7	1.6	2.1	1.6	1.5	1.4
Deutschemark	4.0	14.3	14.0	19.4	17.5	16.5	14.8
French franc	0.2	0.5	0.4	0.5	0.6	0.8	0.7
Swiss franc	0.9	1.7	1.4	1.0	1.4	1.1	1.0
Netherlands guilder	0.2	0.7	0.6	1.0	1.1	1.1	1.0
Japanese yen	0.2	3.3	6.3	8.8	8.2	6.6	5.8
Unspecified currencies	6.2	1.2	1.2	1.1	1.2	1.8	19.4

Developing countries							
US dollar	70.8	59.8	64.9	62.8	62.0	59.4	59.1
Pound sterling	6.8	5.0	4.4	4.4	4.6	5.0	5.0
Deutschemark	8.8	15.5	9.7	9.9	10.8	10.9	10.8
French franc	2.0	2.9	1.7	2.2	2.2	2.0	2.0
Swiss franc	2.3	4.7	2.8	2.9	2.8	2.8	2.4
Netherlands guilder	1.3	1.9	0.9	1.0	1.2	1.1	1.1
Japanese yen	0.9	5.3	5.0	6.7	6.8	7.9	7.8
Unspecified currencies	7.1	4.9	10.6	10.3	9.4	10.9	11.4

Notes: * Starting with 1979, the SDR value of ECUs issued against dollars is added to the SDR value of dollars, but the SDR value of ECUs issued against gold is excluded from the total distributed here. Only selected countries that provide information about the currency composition of their official holdings of foreign exchange are included in this table. † This column is for comparison and indicates the currency composition of reserves when holdings of ECUs are treated as a separate reserve asset, unlike the earlier columns starting with 1979 as is explained in the preceding footnotes. The share of ECUs in total foreign-exchange holdings was 11.7 per cent for all countries and 18.7 per cent for the industrial countries in 1987.

Source: IMF, Annual Report, 1988.

1984 to just above 59 per cent in 1987 as a combined result of valuation effects and outright portfolio diversification.

(*iii*) *Store of value in financial markets*   Dollar-denominated assets held by private foreign investors are recorded in Eurocurrency and international bond market statistics. The latest data points to a lower relative importance of the dollar and growing currency diversification. Reporting banks' cross-border (dollar) assets, even when expressed in value terms, grew in 1987 at a more subdued rate than in 1986, following two years of sharp increases, while the growth of claims in other currencies accelerated significantly, outpacing for the first time (in absolute value) that of dollar assets. Hence the share of these in total outstanding cross-border assets declined. The change was more pronounced when measured in current dollar terms; the share fell from 72 per cent in 1984 to 58 per cent in 1986 and to just below 52 per cent in 1987.

As for international bonds outstanding, the share of dollar issues declined markedly and continuously from 57 per cent in 1985, to 51 per cent in 1986 and 43 per cent in 1987.

If one considers net new borrowing in international bond markets, the figures, adjusted for exchange rate effects, indicate a significant decrease in the dollar fraction of total net issues.

4.2. Will the dollar dominance be preserved?

The empirical evidence surveyed in the previous section suggests that the dominant position of the dollar in world markets has declined somewhat in recent years. Some movement toward a multiple-currency system has indeed occurred. The future evolution in the role of the dollar will depend on the extent to which it will be able to maintain its 'key-currency' characteristics and on the emergence of possible substitutes for the American currency.

The latter question will not be considered here. On the former, the essential attributes of an international currency are exchange convenience and capital certainty. In regard to the first attribute, the largest share of world goods trade is still transacted (and invoiced) in dollars; furthermore, there is evidence that the role of the dollar as means of payments in capital transactions has expanded. From the standpoint of capital certainty the US market for domestic securities is still much broader in size, more diversified, and more liquid than competing markets in other leading countries;

for example, the total value of security issues in the USA is still larger than the sum total of the two next most important markets, Japan and Germany. On the other hand, fluctuations in the dollar rate in recent years have been considerably wider than in other major currencies, resulting in greater potential or actual losses by international portfolio holders. Over the medium term, therefore, the US market may no longer continue to be the preferred habitat of private international investors. Thus the tendency to a decline of the dollar's role as store of value in financial markets, evidenced by the figures on Eurocurrency and international bond de-nominations (see Section 4.1), may gain further momentum.

The position of the USA has no historical antecedents; it has become an increasingly large net debtor while the dollar has so far broadly maintained its role as international currency. Other coun-tries do not provide a relevant parallel. Britain's, and Sterling's, role in the world economy declined in step with its net foreign asset position; the process, though, was gradual and in the aftermath of the Second World War the country was still a net creditor. Issuers of minor reserve currencies, such as the yen and D-mark, have also been creditors. Hence, only fairly general conjectures can be made in regard to the above set of questions.

On one side are the benefits and costs to the USA of preserving the key role of the dollar. The USA has enjoyed a gain from seigniorage, i.e. it has been able to run a greater cumulative deficit (absorption in excess of domestic production) than otherwise possible and has benefitted from added degrees of freedom in its macro-policy options, for example, opting for financing of the deficit rather than domestic adjustment.

The benefits have been matched by the related costs: i) the rate of interest paid to foreign holders of claims on the USA which is an increasing function of the degree of international currency competition, and of the risk exposure of foreign portfolio holders as the share of net claims on the USA in their total wealth rises; ii) the constraints on domestic policies which tend to increase with the size of stock positions taken by foreign investors.[20]

On the other side benefits and risks for the rest of the world have to be recognized and assessed.

We referred above to the primacy of the US domestic market in terms of size, variety of financial instruments, liquidity, etc. The continuing trend toward portfolio diversification and greater cross-border mobility of capital has so far generated a stronger demand for dollar holdings, but with liberalization of capital controls and financial innovation in competing centres (Japan, Germany, and others) alternative outlets have emerged for world portfolios.

On the question of the limits to exchange risk exposure on dollar-denominated assets in the face of large currency losses due to the dollar slide, the Japanese case provides partial but useful information.[21] Since 1984 Japanese portfolio investment abroad soared,[22] and roughly half of it was directed toward US securities. Institutional investors, in particular, stepped up acquisitions of foreign securities as restrictions on capital outflows were gradually relaxed. These investors, notably life-insurance companies and pension funds, reportedly are interested in pursuing longer-term investment strategies, for example holding bonds to maturity. Thus, they view yield differentials in favour of US securities as providing a reasonable protection over the long term against exchange risk. In addition, since the degree of foreign currency exposure is still relatively low for many institutions,[23] it is expected to rise in the future, hence capital outflows to the USA are likely to continue. *Ceteris paribus*, the recent appreciation of the yen, by driving down the share of foreign securities in total assets, should increase investors' demand for dollar-denominated assets.

Notes

[1] This definition is found in Islam (1987). It has the undoubted advantage of symmetry and non-arbitrariness as to the presumed liquidity of claims used as collateral against gross foreign debt. As Islam notes, in the discussion of LDC debt net debt is commonly defined as gross debt minus those claims on foreigners that are considered liquid and readily accessible (typically, official reserves and commercial banks' foreign assets).

[2] Historically, the United States had been a capital importer for most of the period following independence; according to reasonable estimates (see Solomon, 1985), external debt reached a peak of around 25 per cent relative to GNP in 1873 concomitantly with the massive expansion of investment in infrastructure and industry. In subsequent years the US became a capital exporter and continued to be one until the 1970s; from 1914 it was a net creditor.

[3] The official balance-of-payments statistics indicate a sharp slowdown

in acquisition by US residents of assets overseas rather than a sizeable increase in US liabilities; the dollar appreciation has thus been predicated by some observers not on an increase in capital inflows, but rather on a decrease in US demand for foreign currencies, as suggested by the data. However, once the figures are corrected for inter-bank flows and the establishment of International Banking Facilities in December 1981 and early 1982, the picture is one of moderately slowing growth in US private claims on the rest of the world since 1981 and of increasing foreign claims on the USA, particularly in 1984. For a careful analysis see Isard and Stekler (1985).

[4] The simplified procedure adopted for adjusting the NIIP in Table 3 also assumes that the valuation effects on the unrecorded stocks can be safely ignored. For a more detailed discussion of this problem, see Islam (1984).

[5] The IMF and OECD medium-term projections forecast US current deficits persistently above $100 billion throughout 1992.

[6] The stock and flow views are not completely independent, because the size of the externally held stock is apt to influence the size and sustainability of the flow demand.

[7] The shift in attitudes toward the path of the dollar by US policy makers before and after the Plaza Agreement in 1985 is revealing in this regard.

[8] This view lies outside the scope of this paper, as it is chiefly concerned with the increase in foreign direct investment in the USA as a separate question from that of the accumulation of foreign debt. The notion of the possible loss of sovereignty caused by foreign capital has gained a popular audience in the USA. For an intelligent articulation of this view, see the following comments by Rohatyn (1988): 'What is at stake is not only the loss of our position as the leader of the Western democracies, but the loss of our independence of action both in economic and in foreign policy. . . . Our increasing dependence on foreign capital is not just an economic issue. It is also a security issue, as well as a political issue with major implications for foreign and domestic policy. The extent to which the USA is a prisoner of foreign capital becomes apparent when we consider three facts: our net foreign debt is now the largest in the world; the outflow of financial payments is greater than the inflow; the dollar is at, or near, its lowest level since World War II.'

[9] A comparison of the present status of the USA as a capital importer and net debtor with the historical experience of other countries is offered by Marris (1985), chapter 2.

[10] The highlight of the projections, or reference scenarios, is the persistence of large external imbalances for the major countries (United States, Japan, and Germany). A not-too-dissimilar set of results was obtained

by the IMF. For a more detailed presentation, see Gomel *et al.* (1988).

[11] Nominal output in the USA grows at 6 per cent per year from 1993 to 2000; exports grow at 8 per cent; the nominal interest rate on US external liabilities is 7 per cent.

[12] The stock of foreign debt (NIIP) would amount to $1.7 trillion. Similar orders of magnitude can be found in Islam (1984).

[13] This hypothesis—which may look too optimistic—is critical; it entails a current deficit which is a decreasing share of GNP. Under different assumptions (e.g., US current account, hence net acquisition of claims by foreigners at an annual rate equivalent to the actual 1987 magnitudes, i.e., about $150 billion or 3.5 per cent of GNP), foreign debt would reach 40 per cent of GNP by the end of the century or about $4 trillion in absolute value. These figures would represent some 5-6 per cent of total net wealth in the rest of the OECD area. Under such a scenario, even the official 'optimism' falters: 'Relative to the size of the economy, US net indebtedness would not be much larger than Canada's has been in recent years. However, the absolute figure would be very large. This could present difficulties for the world financial system, especially if for some reason foreigners suddenly become less willing to hold claims on the USA' (Economic Report of the President, February 1988).

[14] This case is nicely stated by Islam (1984, p. 22): 'The USA pays for its purchases of foreign goods, services and capital not by first obtaining scarce foreign exchange through bank borrowing or foreign currency bonds, but by simply writing a check in dollars. If the foreign recipients of dollar payments do not find others willing to absorb the excess dollars in the form of some dollar (US or non-US) assets at the prevailing exchange and interest rates, then the dollar may fall and interest rates rise.'

[15] The statistical picture in Table 7 is incomplete. Over the 1970s and up to 1982 a sizeable flow of dollars originated from large non-oil LDC deficits; at the same time massive OPEC surpluses generated a demand for dollars. Since the inception of the debt crisis, however, this pattern of deficits and surpluses has sharply changed; according to 1987 figures, supply and demand from these two areas are of small size and in exact balance.

[16] The discrepancy between these figures and those reported in the US balance of payments which show a $48 billion increase in foreign official assets in the USA arises from placements of official balances in the USA through private institutions or outside the USA in the form of Eurodollar deposits and securities issued in the Euromarkets (see note 19).

[17] This is unlikely to recur. First, developing countries may actually attempt to reduce the dollar share of their reserve holdings. Second,

and most importantly, further increases in official dollar reserves in G10 countries may lead to conflicts with domestic targets of monetary policy.

[18] See Kenen (1983), p. 8.

[19] The data published by the IMF is rather difficult to interpret and only in part accurate. The statistics on the currency composition of foreign exchange are compiled on the basis of surveys and estimates derived mainly from national reports. But some central banks do not report fully their holdings or some holdings are not included in their reserves. An illustration of the phenomenon is provided by the foreign central banks' financing of the US current account deficit in 1987. Foreign official dollar assets in the USA rose by $47.5 billion, thereby covering about 30 per cent of the US deficit. Such funds are duly recorded as an increase in US liabilities towards foreign official institutions in the US balance of payments. But large official dollar balances were placed in the USA through private banks and securities houses or in the form of securities issued by US borrowers in the Euromarkets. These official funds appeared as a large unallocated item in the US balance of payments of over $60 billion (see BIS, Annual Report 1988).

[20] This is usually referred to as 'debt overhang'. It is described in the following terms by Salant as early as 1964: 'If a country performs international banking functions and its debt takes the form of deposits payable on demand, its customers' decisions whether to increase or decrease their deposits may determine whether it borrows or repays short-term debt. The decisions depend largely on the depositors' views as to the attractiveness of the reserve currency as compared with alternative reserve assets.' The potentially disruptive risks associated with the debt overhang are well known to anyone recognizing that financial market are driven by states of 'confidence' and volatile changes in expectations.

[21] Total Japanese assets in the USA account for roughly 12 per cent of foreign assets; for bonds, the share is 14 per cent.

[22] Japanese purchases of foreign securities increased from $31 billion in 1984 to over $100 billion in 1986 and nearly $90 billion in 1987. For a detailed discussion, see Kawai and Okumura (1988).

[23] The average ratio of foreign to total securities was 3 per cent in 1980, 9 per cent in 1984, and 17 per cent in 1987.

References

Bank for International Settlements, Annual Report, various issues.

Cohen, B. (1971), *The Future of Sterling as an International Currency* (Macmillan, London).

Friedman, B. (1986), *Implications of the US Net Capital Inflow* (NBER Working Paper, January).

—— (1988*a*), 'The Campaign's Hidden Issue', *The New York Review of Books*, 13 October.

—— (1988*b*), *Day of Reckoning: The Consequences of American Economic Policy under Reagan and After* (Random House, New York).

Gomel, G., Marchese, G., and J. C. Martinez Oliva (1989), *The Adjustment of the US Current Account Imbalance: The Role of International Policy Coordination* (Bank of Italy, Temi di Discussione, July).

International Monetary Fund, Annual Report, various issues.

Isard, P. and L. Stekler (1985), 'US International Capital Flows and the Dollar', *Brookings Papers on Economic Activity*, no. 1.

Islam, S. (1984), 'Foreign Debt of the United States and the Dollar', *FRB of New York Research Paper*, no. 8415 (September).

—— (1987), 'America's Foreign Debt: is the Debt Crisis Moving North?', *Stanford Journal of International Law*, vol. 23.

—— (1988), *America's Foreign Debt: Fear, Fantasy, Fiction and Facts* (Congressional Research Service Workshop, Washington).

Kawai, M. and H. Okumura (1988), *Japan's Portfolio Investment in Foreign Securities* (Japan Center for International Finance, Policy Study Series, no. 9, January).

Kenen, P. (1983), *The Role of the Dollar as an International Currency* (Group of Thirty, New York).

Krugman, P. (1985), 'Is the Strong Dollar Sustainable?', in *The US Dollar—Recent Developments, Outlook and Policy Options*, Symposium by the Federal Reserve Bank of Kansas City.

—— (1987), 'Sustainability and the Decline of the Dollar', *Brookings Discussion Papers in International Economics* (March).

Marris, S. (1985), *Deficits and the Dollar: the World Economy at Risk* (Institute for International Economics, Washington).

—— (1987), *Deficits and the Dollar Revisited: August 1987* (Institute for International Economics, Washington).

Organisation for Economic Cooperation and Development, Economic Outlook, various issues.

Rohatyn, F. (1988), *The New York Review of Books* 18 February.

Roosa, R. (1965), *Monetary Reform for the World Economy* (Harper & Row, New York).

Salant, W. (1964), 'The Reserve Currency Role of the Dollar: Blessing or Burden to the United States?', *Review of Economics and Statistics*, no. 2 (May).

Solomon, R. (1985*a*), 'The US as a Debtor in the 19th Century', *Brookings Discussion Papers in International Economics* (May).

—— (1985*b*), 'Effects of the Strong Dollar', *Brookings Discussion Papers in International Economics* (September).

Triffin, R. (1960), *Gold and the Dollar Crisis* (Yale University Press, New Haven).

US Department of Commerce (1988), *United States Trade Performance in 1987* (June).

van der Ven, G. and J. Wilson (1986), 'The United States International Asset and Liability Position: a Comparison of Flow of Funds and Commerce Department Presentations', *FRB International Finance Discussion Papers* (November).

Whitman, M. (1974), 'The Current and Future Role of the Dollar: How Much Symmetry?', *Brookings Papers on Economic Activity*, no. 3.

How Have Exchange Rate Fluctuations Affected US Prices?

SPECIAL MERIT AWARD

Editors' Introduction

In this essay Robert Feinberg of the American University reports on the important results of his recent extensive statistical work on exchange rates and prices. Studies of the effect of international shocks on US import and domestic prices have found relatively limited 'passthrough'. He argues that one reason for this absence of the expected influence of exchange rates on inflation is the use of an inappropriate currency index. The essay concludes that the commonly used Federal Reserve Board index, based on only ten countries, overstates the extent of the dollar's fluctuations against its trading partners' currencies. Hence the apparent low 'passthrough' in part results from the currency change being less than assumed. A wider index, such as the Federal Reserve Bank of Dallas index, is a better measure of US competitiveness and of the true extent of the dollar's fluctuations. Better still are industry-specific indices, which show that some US manufacturers are in a far worse competitive position than previously thought.

Robert M. Feinberg, 38, is an Associate Professor at the American University in Washington DC. Between 1987 and 1989 he was Senior Economist at the US International Trade Commission, to which he remains a consultant. In 1979–80 he was Visiting Economist at the US Justice Department. He received his Ph.D from the University of Virginia and his B.A. from the University of Pennsylvania. From 1976 until 1987 Dr Feinberg was Assistant and Associate Professor at The Pennsylvania State University. He has published frequently in leading academic journals, including the *Review of Economics and Statistics*, *Kyklos*, and the *Journal of Industrial Economics*.

3

How Have Exchange Rate Fluctuations Affected US Prices?

ROBERT M. FEINBERG

The past 15 years of exchange rate fluctuations have encouraged economists to study the effects of exchange-rate movements on US import and domestic prices. These effects tell us how insulated American consumers and producers are from international shocks; at the same time, they represent a partial indicator of the influence of international monetary and financial management on the domestic market. Generally, these effects have been found to be surprisingly small, especially in the short run, with less than 75 per cent of the magnitude of exchange-rate changes passed through into US import prices and less than 20 per cent of the magnitude of exchange rate changes passed through into domestic prices.

After briefly discussing explanations for this limited 'passthrough', this essay will focus on one of them: the mis-measurement of exchange rate movements. Virtually all economic studies of 'passthrough' have used as the measure of US exchange rate change, the ten-country multilateral-trade-weighted exchange rate indices compiled by the Federal Reserve Board (FED), or a similarly narrowly based aggregate index. If much of US foreign trade occurs with countries other than those included in the index, in the aggregate and for particular industries, such an index will not accurately reflect movements in the effective terms of trade.

Of course, if all exchange rates against the dollar had moved together, it would not matter which exchange rate index was used to answer the question posed in the title of this essay. But, by comparing movements in FED, a different, very broad (101 country) index compiled at the Federal Reserve Bank of Dallas (DALLAS), and eighty-one industry-specific exchange rate indices over the 1973–88 period, this essay shows that the choice of index does matter. Both the magnitude of change in exchange rates and the degree of estimated 'passthrough' into domestic prices are shown to differ by exchange rate index employed.

1. What Determines Passthrough?

While much of the economic and financial 'passthrough' literature examines the effect of exchange rates on import prices, or of import prices on domestic prices, the focus of this essay is on the total impact of currency movements on domestic producer prices. How do currency movements affect domestic prices? As the dollar appreciates, foreign firms find that it is less costly (in dollar terms) to serve the US market, at constant foreign costs measured in their local currency; this means that the supply of imports to the USA increases, lowering import prices and putting downward pressure on domestic prices of goods competitive with imports—this can be thought of as the 'demand' effect of exchange-rate changes. In addition, domestic firms which can use imported inputs find that these inputs are lower-priced, reducing their costs of production and allowing for further domestic price reductions on the final products they sell—this can be thought of as the 'supply' effect of exchange-rate changes.

In considering the initial foreign-supply responses to exchange rate changes, we must realize that these are determined both by nominal exchange rates and by relative inflationary pressures, implying that it is the real value of foreign exchange rate movements that matters. In other words, if the dollar appreciates from 200 Yen to 300 Yen, but Japanese prices all increase by 50 per cent, there will be no change in the Japanese producers' ability to serve the US market.

Changes in the real external value of the US dollar since the early 1970s, measured by FED, have recently been found to have passed most fully into domestic prices of industries heavily reliant on imported inputs and producing goods highly substitutable for imports.[1] Capital-intensive and concentrated industries and those protected by barriers to entry—to both domestic and foreign competitors—exhibited less domestic price change from exchange-rate movements. On average only 16 per cent of the magnitude of exchange-rate movements were passed into domestic prices.

Consider some explanations for the minimal amount of pass-through observed. These include imperfect substitutability between imports and domestic products, and small proportions of imported inputs (in explaining low passthrough into domestic prices), market power by exporters (in explaining low passthrough into import prices), general macroeconomic considerations, and inadequacy of data.

To the extent that the products imported are not in competition with home production, exchange rate-driven changes in import prices will have little effect on the pricing decisions of domestic manufacturers; similarly, if the great proportion of the value of domestic production is accounted for by domestic labour and materials, changes in the cost of imported inputs will have little effect on domestic prices. In addition, if foreign exporters have sufficient market power to adjust their profit margins in response to currency movements, without significantly changing import prices, there will be little reason for prices of domestic merchandise to change.

At a more complex level, exchange rates change largely because of macroeconomic policies (both at home and abroad), meaning that the effect of exchange rates on prices cannot always be easily isolated from the effect of the underlying monetary and fiscal policies on prices. Finally, if exchange rates are changing by more or less than we think they are, our estimated price-responses to these mismeasured exchange rates will themselves be biased; this last issue is discussed below.

2. How Much Has the Real Exchange Rate Changed?

To investigate how differing trade patterns across industries would affect the exchange rate pressures faced by US producers, census data was used to calculate annual industry-specific real exchange rate indices (IND) for eighty-one US industries over the 1973–88 period.[2]

The magnitude of real appreciation of the dollar from its mid-period low point (generally in 1978 or 1979) to the peak[3] (in 1985 or 1986) was 59 per cent as measured by FED, 38 per cent as measured by DALLAS and ranged from 26 per cent to 77 per cent by the industry-specific measures, IND (with an unweighted mean appreciation of 41 per cent). The depreciation, to 1988, was 33 per cent measured by FED, 21 per cent measured by DALLAS, and ranged from 6 to 34 per cent, for IND (with an unweighted mean depreciation of 21 per cent).

Of greater interest, from the perspective of the long-run competitive position of US producers against competing imports, is the extent to which the real value of the dollar has returned to its pre-appreciation level;[4] a sustained real appreciation implies that the purchase of foreign goods requires less sacrifice of domestic goods than previously (and, similarly, domestic goods require for their purchase abroad more of a sacrifice of foreign goods, thus inhibiting exports). The depreciation, to 1988, in FED was 89 per cent of what was required to offset the previous appreciation, suggesting that US manufacturers should be in a fairly strong position to compete against imports in their home market. However, the depreciation in DALLAS was only 76 per cent of that required, and IND fell by between 16 and 116 per cent (on average 75 per cent), of what was required to offset the previous appreciation in their real effective terms of trade.

Why has FED diverged from the other indices? In particular, why has FED understated the extent to which the real terms of trade in the US market have moved against American manufacturing? There are three explanations: (1) outdated weights; (2) incomplete country-coverage; and (3) a multilateral-trade versus bilateral-trade weighting scheme.

FED is based on trade weights reflecting world-wide exports and imports in 1972, for ten countries which accounted for about 65 per cent of US non-oil imports in both 1974 and 1986, and a smaller percentage of total US trade (exports and imports), while DALLAS considers current trade weights and reflects the exchange-rate movements of 101 US trading partners accounting for 97.5 per cent of US trade. At first glance, FED may seem as representative of US import competition today as in the mid-seventies; the share of US non-petroleum imports accounted for by the ten countries included in the index is roughly 65 per cent in both 1974 and 1986. However, the composition of imports from those ten has changed substantially, with the relative importance of Japan and Canada—two countries whose real exchange rates have not moved in step with those in Western Europe—much different in the late eighties from what is suggested by the weighting scheme of the index.

The weights in FED are based on multilateral trade (i.e., each country's share of world-wide trade), while those in DALLAS and IND are bilateral (reflecting only trade with the USA); this leads to an over-emphasis in FED on European currency movements since the great volume of intra-European trade leads to inflated weights for the eight European countries contained in that index, and an understatement of the importance of Canadian exchange-rate movements, since so large a share of Canada's trade is with the USA (but their share of world-wide trade is relatively small). For example, FED assigns over 77 per cent of its weight to the eight European countries, 9 per cent to Canada, and 14 per cent to Japan; in terms of US non-oil imports (for 1986), however, Canada has 19 per cent, Japan has 25 per cent, and the eight European countries have 23 per cent.

Those industries showing the greatest adverse effect of the long cycle of appreciation and depreciation, in terms of an insufficient depreciation in their industry-specific real exchange rates include:

● rice, cotton broad-woven fabrics, women's, girls' and infants' apparel, and gloves—dominated by imports from the Asian developing countries;
● cane and beet sugar, and cigars—dominated by imports from the Caribbean and Latin American nations;
● cottonseed oil, ceramic bricks, ceramic plumbing fixtures, and concrete block and brick—dominated by imports from Mexico; and
● tufted floor coverings, lumber, wood-pulp, explosives, concrete block and brick, gypsum products, and steel springs—dominated by imports from Canada.

3. How Have Domestic Prices Responded to the Exchange Rate Changes?

Using statistical estimation techniques, I now consider the next step—the magnitude of passthrough from real exchange rates into relative domestic producer prices of traded goods.

Conceptually, a two-stage procedure is involved: (1) a response specific to each industry between the real exchange rate and relative producer prices is estimated; and (2) the differences across industries in the estimated response are explained by a series of industry variables, intended to measure domestic competitive conditions, the nature of substitutability between domestic and imported goods, non-tariff barriers to trade, import penetration, and the importance of imported inputs to the domestic industry. All three measures of the real exchange rate, FED, DALLAS, and IND, are evaluated.

Using any of the three exchange rate measures, a major determinant of producer price movements in the US from 1974 to 1987 was the external value of the dollar. Restricting the price response to exchange rates to be the same across all industries gives a rough average effect, which may be compared for the three real exchange rate indices. Using FED, a response coefficient of 0.16 is obtained; that is, an appreciation of 10 per cent in the real external value of the dollar is predicted to lower producer prices for the industries in the sample relative to overall inflation by 1.6 per cent on average by the following year. However, the much broader DALLAS yields a higher coefficient of 0.27, suggesting that the use of FED may significantly understate estimates of domestic price responses to exchange rates.

One's expectation would be that the industry-specific exchange rate indices (IND), based on actual patterns of import competition, would generate still stronger passthrough; however, this is not the case, with the restricted passthrough coefficient only slightly higher, at 0.17, than that obtained with FED. Before exploring the industry determinants of differences in passthough, some discussion is required to explain this apparent anomaly.

IND would certainly seem to better measure demand-side pressures on domestic prices from currency movements than either FED or DALLAS. However, domestic cost pressures, varying with the importance of imported inputs to an industry, are a major force in influencing domestic price response to exchange-rate movements; and the most broadly based index, DALLAS, may better pick up changes in the prices of widely available imported inputs than IND,[5] while being something of a compromise candidate in measuring demand-side (import-competition) effects.

Now, let us turn to the explanation of different price responses across industries. Exchange rate passthrough into domestic prices should be explained by variables relating to domestic competition factors and the ease of entry into the domestic market, import penetration, the substitutability of foreign for domestic goods, and the sensitivity of domestic costs to exchange rate movements. Of course, to the extent that trade barriers exist in particular industries, consumers may be unable to substitute foreign for domestic products as one would otherwise predict; this would limit the effect of exchange-rate changes on domestic prices.

Several results are consistent across all three measures of real exchange-rate movements: (1) the cost-share of imported inputs, and capital intensity seem to play especially important roles in influencing the passthrough of exchange rates into domestic prices, imported inputs enhancing and capital intensity limiting the exchange rate effects; (2) increased market power tends to limit somewhat the responsiveness of domestic prices to exchange rates: and (3) increased substitutability between domestic and imported goods increases the passthrough, though limited by non-tariff barriers to imports.

The issue of demand (import competition) versus supply (imported inputs) effects on passthrough, noted above, can be addressed by comparing the effects of import/domestic good substitutability and of imported input cost on the price response obtained by using, alternately, IND and DALLAS. Consider doubling the substitutability of imports for domestic product (in the absence of non-tariff barriers); this increases the passthrough effect by 25 per cent more when currency movements are measured by IND— more accurately reflecting demand-side pressures from substitutable imports—than when DALLAS is used. On the other hand, a doubling in the share of costs attributed to imported inputs increases the passthrough effect by 20 per cent more when DALLAS—most likely to capture movements in the cost of imported inputs—is used than when IND is used. This demonstrates that the choice of exchange rate index not only determines the observed passthrough into domestic prices; it also influences judgements as to what factors cause the passthrough to differ across industries.

4. Conclusion

This essay has examined the relationship between alternative measures of currency-value fluctuations and domestic producer prices. Changes in the real external value of the US dollar since the start of floating rates in the mid-1970s have passed most fully into domestic prices of industries heavily reliant on imported inputs and producing goods highly substitutable for imports. Capital-intensive and concentrated industries and those protected

by barriers to entry—to both domestic and foreign competitors—
have exhibited less domestic price change from exchange-rate
movements. These results seem robust to the choice of an exchange-
rate index.

In addition, the evidence suggests that the combination of
demand- and supply-side pressures on domestic prices due to
currency-value movements cannot be adequately measured by a
single index. Supply (or cost) pressures are most successfully
captured by a broad aggregate index, and demand (or import-
competition) pressures are explained best by an industry-specific
index.

Finally, the extent of both real appreciation and real depreciation
in the external value of the dollar since the late seventies has been
overstated for most industries by the Federal Reserve Board's
ten-country index, and is better measured by the Dallas Fed's
101-country index. The extent to which the recent depreciation has
offset the earlier period of appreciation has also been overstated
by the narrower Board index. The Dallas Fed's index suggests that
average US competitiveness is somewhat worse than is indicated
by the Board index. Furthermore, industry-specific indices suggest
that a number of US manufacturers are in a far worse competitive
position *vis-à-vis* the rest of the world than previously thought.

Notes

[1] See Robert M. Feinberg (1989), 'The Effects of Foreign Exchange
Movements on US Domestic Prices', *The Review of Economics and
Statistics* (August).

[2] Country shares of US imports for each industry were averaged for 1978,
1981, and 1984. The International Monetary Fund database was used
to obtain consumer price indices and exchange rates (against the dollar)
for the thirty-one countries with a 10 per cent share of imports for at
least one of the eighty-one industries analysed. Real exchange rate
indices (1973 = 100) were calculated for each of these thirty-one
countries. Geometric weighted averages (using the country-share weights)
were then calculated to yield the eighty-one real exchange rate indices,
with countries having import shares less than 10 per cent grouped
together and assigned the broad 101-country index referred to above
(DALLAS). See the discussion introducing this index in W. Michael
Cox, 'A Comprehensive New Real Dollar Exchange Rate Index', *Federal
Reserve Bank of Dallas Economic Review* (March), 1–14.

³ It should be kept in mind that these exchange rate indices are annual averages; thus, 'peak' values will be lower than the true peak values calculated from, say, a daily index. This implies that all the indices discussed here will underestimate the magnitude of both appreciation and depreciation.

⁴ It should be noted that the percentage depreciation required to bring a given percentage appreciation down to its initial level is smaller than the percentage appreciation. In general, an appreciation of x per cent will be fully offset by a depreciation of $y = x/(1+(x/100))$ per cent. For example, an appreciation of 41 per cent will be fully offset by a depreciation of 29 per cent.

⁵ This will be true unless the sources of a particular industry's imported inputs are the same as the sources of competing final good imports.

Globalization and Economic Policy Formulation

SPECIAL MERIT AWARD

Editors' Introduction

This essay by Paul Mortimer-Lee of the Bank of England surveys the causes and consequences of the globalization of financial markets. The increasing 'interconnectedness and interdependence' of world financial markets has happened in response to the demand for financial flows to support growing international trade and investment and because of the emergence of large imbalances. At the same time, the ability to supply financial services at a reasonable cost was made possible due to advances in technology.

The main consequence of globalization is that countries have less independence in policy-making. The better working of the market on an international basis quickly disciplines any action which is seen to be adverse. While the author admits that some aspects of globalization might prove costly, overall the world benefits. The essay argues that globalization of financial markets will lead to a closer convergence of economic policies between countries, but concludes that formal co-ordination is not necessary as a well-functioning market should fill that role.

Paul Mortimer-Lee, 36, obtained his B.Sc. (Economics) and M.Sc. from the London School of Economics. He joined the Bank of England in 1976 and worked there as an economist and economic forecaster. He was seconded to the International Monetary Fund between 1982 and 1984, where he was in the African Department. He now works as a Senior Manager in the Gilt-Edged Division of the Bank of England.

4

Globalization and Economic Policy Formulation

PAUL MORTIMER-LEE*

One of the most important and striking developments of the last quarter century has been the increasing interconnectedness and interdependence of world financial markets. This greater globalization is reflected in the reporting of economic events, in an increased concentration on economic developments abroad and on developments in international financial markets. Its extent and importance was demonstrated most dramatically in the world-wide fall in stock-market prices in October 1987.

The trend towards globalization raises many wide-ranging issues for investors, borrowers, governments and central banks, amongst others. The current essay concentrates on one particular area, and asks the question: 'Why has globalization of financial markets occurred and what are its consequences for economic policies?'

The answer to this question is provided in four parts: first, we have tried to understand better what globalization is and why it has arisen; second, we have examined the limitations of independent monetary policy implied by globalization; third, we have examined some of the benefits globalization brings, and the problems it requires policy-makers to overcome; fourth, and finally, we have drawn some conclusions about where globalization is leading. Other important topics, such as the implications of globalization for prudential supervision, are beyond the scope of this paper.

1. What is globalization and why has it arisen?

Globalization of financial markets is a fact, and in the absence of catastrophic events probably an irreversible one: it behoves us to understand what it is and why it exists.

* This essay was stimulated by the 1989 Salzburg Seminar on 'Internationalization of Financial Markets'. I am also grateful for helpful comments from J. S. Flemming. The views in this essay are entirely those of the author and do not necessarily reflect those of the Bank of England.

Table 1 Estimated net lending in international markets: 1983–1988 (US$ billions; banking flows adjusted to exclude estimated exchange rate effects)

	1983	1984	1985	1986	1987	1988
1. Gross international bank lending	126	152	297	654	760	495
2. Net international bank lending	85	90	105	195	300	225
3. Gross new bond issues*	74	109	165	222	181	219
4. Less redemptions and repurchases	14	25	39	59	71	81
5. New new bond issues	60	84	126	162	110	138
6. Net new euronote placements	—	6	10	13	23	20
7. Total international financing (2 + 5 + 6)	145	180	241	370	433	383
8. Less double counting	13	28	55	83	53	68
9. Total net international financing	132	152	186	287	380	315

Notes: * On a completions basis.

Source: BIS, Bank of England and Euroclear.

The main feature of globalization is an increase in the interdependence of the world's financial markets. Table 1 shows the pattern of flows in the international markets in the period since 1983. The BIS estimates that the stock of net international financing increased from $1,500 billion at end-1983 to a massive $3,200 billion at end-1988. Interdependence existed in the past, as is clear when one recalls that international capital flows were the proximate causes of exchange rate crises under the Bretton Woods system; it is the current scale and fluidity of international financial market linkages rather than their existence that are unusual by reference to post-war experience. Current developments parallel the experience between 1850 and 1914 when international financial linkages strengthened considerably, a process reversed by the two world wars and the intervening depression and tighter exchange controls. For example, between 1870 and 1910 the net foreign investment of the UK absorbed about $4\frac{1}{4}$ per cent of GNP and a third of the nation's savings; France and Germany were also significant exporters of capital.

The world stock-market fall in October 1987 illustrated the strong links between the main equity markets. However, the phenomenon of globalization extends well beyond these and is stronger in those areas where financial products are more standardized. For example, developments in the US Treasury bond market have important implications for bond markets elsewhere in the world as traders and investors decide whether or not to switch between instruments. Foreign exchange market linkages are so tight—thanks to the actions of traders and arbitrageurs—that it is quite simply a global market, the location of which moves around the world with the hands of the clock.

One reason for the greater interdependence of price movements in world markets in recent years is that investors have greatly increased their holdings of foreign assets, a process which has benefitted from and stimulated the move to greater securitization. Foreign currency borrowing has also increased substantially and non-dollar currencies now feature more in international bond issues (see Table 2). Economic 'news' and changes in expectations now lead investors to alter their behaviour in several markets, not just one as formerly. Financial intermediaries also have expanded their involvement in foreign financial centres, with more and larger presences abroad, serving the needs of international investors and of corporations (both multinational and domestic).

All those whose financial operations have spread across national and currency boundaries—whether investors, borrowers, or financial intermediaries—are interested in achieving for themselves the best possible financial performance. This means constantly assessing whether opportunities exist to improve returns or reduce risk by switching out of one instrument or currency and into another. For example, if yields on US Treasury bonds increase, traders and investors may decide to buy them and sell the now relatively lower yielding UK or French government bonds (gilts and OATs, respectively), thereby moderating the rise in US Treasury bond yields and pulling up the yield on gilts and OATs. Seizing such opportunities requires more information and the means to process it, which technological innovation in telecommunications and computing has helped to supply. There is also a need to be able to take advantage of developments almost immediately, whether or not they are during the trading hours of one's own domestic market—otherwise the actions of others are likely to move

Table 2. Currency structure of the international bond market (US$ billions)

	Gross new issues†					Stocks		
	1985	1986	1987	1988	1982	1985	1987	1988
Total	163.8	221.7	177.1	225.4	259.1	556.7	990.7	1,085.7
US dollar	98.6	121.6	63.3	83.0	145.5	314.8	425.8	470.2
Swiss franc	14.6	23.1	24.1	26.7	42.6	78.6	157.8	139.3
Japanese yen	12.3	22.3	24.8	20.4	16.5	42.8	122.2	132.7
Deutschemark	11.3	16.3	15.3	23.6	31.4	50.6	99.2	103.7
Sterling	6.4	11.4	15.2	23.4	4.6	19.1	54.8	73.5
ECU*	7.5	7.0	7.6	11.3	3.2	16.5	41.0	46.5
Other	13.1	20.0	26.8	37.0	15.3	34.3	90.0	119.8

Notes: * Excludes bonds issued in borrowers' national markets; † Figures for issues are before allowing for repayments and are on an announcements basis.

Sources: Bank of England, AIBD, and BIS.

prices and close down profitable opportunities—giving rise to the phenomenon of 24-hour global trading.

Explaining the reasons why globalization has spread is at heart the same as explaining the development of any new product or market. In all cases, there are three essential ingredients: the demand for the product; the ability to supply at a reasonable price; and the absence of effective official impediments to the market's development.

As far as globalization is concerned, the increase in demand has come partly from the expansion of international trade and foreign investment (both direct and portfolio) which, for example, increases the demand for foreign exchange transactions, for hedging instruments (such as futures and options), and for foreign currency borrowing—either from banks or in the form of bond issues. It has also reflected global financial imbalances. The oil shocks of the 1970s gave rise to the need to recycle the surpluses of the oil exporters. More recently the USA has attracted funds from abroad to finance the related current account and budget deficits, while residents of countries with current account surpluses, notably Japan and Germany, have needed to find foreign assets to invest in. The greater exchange rate volatility following the breakdown of the Bretton Woods system in the early 1970s and greater sophistication in portfolio management has revealed to many the benefits—in terms of achieving higher returns or lowering risk—of diversifying their portfolios internationally, which the removal of exchange controls has allowed them to realize. This has been bolstered by a trend in many countries towards a greater role for institutional investment rather than personal investment in the management of savings.

On the supply side, technological advances in communications and computers have significantly lowered the costs of supplying and analysing information quickly and of meeting the demands for more sophisticated and diversified financial products. The economies of scale realized when financial intermediaries have expanded by operating abroad may also have lowered costs.

The liberalization of financial markets, for example the abolition of exchange controls in the UK as far back as 1979, has removed distortions, reduced inefficiencies, and enabled suppliers of financial services to meet the upsurge in demand while at the same time increasing competition and serving to reduce costs to borrowers and investors still further.

The relationship between the three main elements behind the phenomenon is a dynamic and complicated one. While the liberalization of markets stimulates globalization it also feeds on it, for example, as countries liberalize to prevent domestic financial markets becoming uncompetitive and business moving offshore; in other words, liberalization and globalization are mutually reinforcing. A world with lower transactions costs is also a more fluid one, creating additional risks and opportunities and adding to the demand for new services and products and stimulating further supply innovation. Also, globalization helps to sustain imbalances—by financing them—while at the same time being sustained by them.

Thus globalization is more organic than mechanical, and is dynamic rather than static; the phenomenon as a whole represents much more than the sum of the parts comprising it. It is therefore difficult for governments to control, particularly as financial activity is internationally mobile and can easily relocate. The result is that increasingly corporations, individuals, and financial intermediaries can raise funds or invest them: at any time; in any place; in any currency; and on any terms that they can find a counterparty to agree to.

The private sector therefore has more power to make the decisions that suit its own needs best: this is the source of both the gains claimed for globalization and the problems it poses for governments and central banks, since the actions that suit the private sector's aims the best may thwart those of the authorities.

Globalization means that the world is no longer a series of separate financial markets; segmentation is breaking down.

For the more standardized products, increasingly there is just one market which operates in different places at different times of the day. For example, US Treasury bonds are traded in Tokyo and London, as well as New York; derivative markets, such as futures and options, are developing electronic links around the world to expand this further. One consequence of globalization is that the actions of a single national government are dissipated throughout the entire world financial system, like a pebble dropped in a very large lake. At the same time, the domestic financial economy's stronger links with the outside world mean that it is increasingly affected by actions abroad.

The reduction in the importance of domestic policies relative to those abroad is particularly important for monetary policy, to which we now turn.

2. Limitations on monetary policy

The manifestation of the effects of globalization on monetary policy will be different according to whether countries have fixed or floating exchange rates. If policy adjustment is required in response to domestic or foreign developments, in the short run fiscal policy is inflexible, so that the exchange rate and / or interest rates must change. If the exchange rate is floating, in principle it could take all the strain with domestic interest rates remaining unchanged. If exchange rates are fixed, interest rate policy has to bear all the burden of adjustment. However, this does not mean that the implications of globalization for domestic monetary policy are necessarily more serious in a fixed-rate regime than in a floating-rate environment.

As a descriptive matter a sharp distinction between fixed and floating rates is partly artificial, since most countries which float aim for some degree of exchange rate stability as a contribution to holding inflation stable or to avoiding disruptive changes in competitiveness; and few exchange rates are so firmly fixed as to rule out any possibility of realignment in the face of profound structural changes. The principal qualitative conclusion is the same in the fixed and floating exchange rate worlds: national monetary independence is curtailed by globalization, though the form in which this manifests itself depends on the exchange rate regime.

From an analytical point of view, in today's interdependent world it makes increasingly less sense to think of monetary policy solely in terms of domestic variables such as interest rates or monetary growth. Globalization has changed the transmission mechanism, in which the exchange rate plays a more important role than hitherto while direct controls (e.g. on credit allocation) have a much smaller role. The theoretical reasons for seeing exchange rates and interest rates as different sides of the monetary-policy coin are clear. Changes in domestic interest rates change the relative rates of return to holding assets denominated in different currencies and therefore have an exchange rate effect. Similarly, changes in exchange rates and exchange rate expectations alter the returns to holding foreign versus domestic assets and therefore have effects on domestic and foreign interest rates. Now that more economic units have more freedom to hold foreign assets or liabilities, these linkages play a more important role in many more decisions than formerly. The effects of globalization on monetary policy can therefore be characterized according to the effect on either domestic interest rates or the exchange rate, or some mixture of the two.

The stocks of domestic financial assets held abroad and foreign financial assets held domestically are very large in relation to trade flows and central bank reserves. Changes in the market's perceptions about policy and economic developments can prompt large shifts in the desired composition of these portfolios. With floating this leads to pressure on exchange rates, whereas with fixed exchange rates gains or losses in central banks' foreign exchange reserves— and ultimately domestic interest rates—take the strain. In both settings the pressures are more intense now than they were earlier because the potential flows across the exchanges are so much bigger. It follows that in the globalized world monetary policy adjusts more to shocks and policy developments abroad than formerly, implying less national monetary independence.

As illustration, consider two countries, A and B, with an absolutely and permanently fixed exchange rate. For all practical purposes there would be a common currency, and the relationship between the two currencies would be the same as currently exists between banknotes of different denominations (e.g. between 20 notes and 5 notes). If financial capital were free to flow between the two countries they could not operate national monetary policies independently of each other. Interest rates in country A could not differ from those in country B—in the same way as at present they cannot differ between London and Manchester—otherwise huge capital flows would result as arbitrageurs sought to make absolutely riskless profits. And by definition the two countries would experience the same exchange rate movements *vis-à-vis* the rest of the world. The use of controls as a means of restoring greater autonomy would be doomed to failure because separate national credit controls could be circumvented by the private sector borrowing offshore.

The effects of monetary policy increasingly are felt outside national boundaries and domestic developments are increasingly affected by monetary policy developments abroad, so that monetary policy making will take on something of a trans-national flavour. The increased co-operation and co-ordination this implies between countries can be accomplished formally between national authorities (which is likely to be more difficult the more dissimilar are the countries in other respects, such as economic structure), and/or through the market mechanism, for example as was the case during the operation of the gold standard.

The process of globalization and liberalization has changed the character of monetary policy in many countries, giving a greater role to international and market influences. As we have seen, this means that there are more limitations on monetary policy than formerly, and one more is worth mentioning. The returns paid on components of broad money are now more strongly linked to market interest rates, for example because interest rate ceilings have been lifted in some countries. Changes in nominal interest rates now alter relative interest rates less than formerly, so that it is now more difficult to affect liquidity, and interest rates now have to change by more to affect liquidity than in a less liberalized world. However, as a partial offset to these effects it should be noted that in other respects monetary policy may be more effective than formerly. The tighter linkages between national financial markets means that changes in domestic interest rates more readily encourage inflows or outflows, which means that monetary policy has more power to affect capital flows/exchange rates. Furthermore, some agents are now more highly geared than formerly—for example US companies, and UK households—so that interest rate changes now have a greater effect on the cash flows of these debtors, and therefore on their spending.

Having identified the consequences of globalization for monetary control, it is appropriate to assess the wider economic policy costs and benefits of globalization.

3. Costs and benefits of globalization

The restriction of freedom unilaterally to determine national monetary policy is important in itself, since the instruments of monetary policy are among the most useful and flexible tools available to the authorities.

The proponents of greater globalization stress the gains from more efficient resource allocation. As with trade in goods, countries with a comparative advantage in financial services can concentrate on supplying them, freeing resources in other countries to produce goods and services where their comparative advantage lies. Moreover, globalization means that residents of countries with profitable investment opportunities in excess of the supply of domestic savings can more easily borrow from countries where profitable investment projects are few in relation to the supply of savings. Thus financial capital flows will enable physical capital to be located where it generates the highest returns: borrowing countries can therefore achieve higher investment and growth with globalized markets than without them, while lenders can earn higher returns than if they were restricted to financing purely domestic investment.

However, some commentators question how real the gains from globalization are in actuality, pointing to the huge volume of international financial transactions in relation to international trade volumes. They ask whether the flows of financial capital actually result in a relocation of real resources, particularly as many factors—such as tax positions, political and economic uncertainties, and short-run changes in relative interest rates—may prompt large flows of short-term financial capital which may easily not correspond with underlying productivity differences. This view is that the international financial markets are in essence a casino and that the massive turnover in financial markets is generated artificially; the result, so the argument runs, is excessive volatility in markets and profits for banks and investment houses.

But financial firms as a group cannot make profits if there are no real customers willing to pay for the services provided. Otherwise, any trading profits of successful financial firms will be offset by losses suffered by others. The banks and investment houses would still have to pay their costs (of technology and staff for example), so that as a group they would make massive and consistent losses, which is unsustainable. Since real customers are willing to pay for the services globalized financial firms provide we must presume they receive real benefits in return.

Even if day-to-day volatility in markets were to increase as a result of globalization it would not necessarily follow that this was undesirable. The reduction in information and processing costs that has accompanied globalization means that markets can track changes in equilibria better, and so the efficiency of resource allocation will improve. Greater volatility as a result of globalization may be a benefit rather than a cost of the process to the extent that it reflects genuine changes in perceptions about future developments, though those affected by increased volatility—stockholders in October 1987, for example—may judge otherwise.

It is argued above that globalization erodes the ability to deploy independent national monetary policy, implying a reduced scope to control economic goals such as GDP or employment. Whether one views this as an advantage or disadvantage depends on how one sees the economy working. Many lament losing what they see as an extra lever with which to help control the real economy. Others take the view that in the longer run (which may be quite short) expansionary monetary policy cannot affect real GDP or employment, but can only have an adverse effect on prices. In this view, globalization has the favourable effect of forcing governments to adopt structural solutions to structural problems at an earlier stage than otherwise, with benefits for long run growth and employment prospects.

Globalization clearly means that capital flows are much bigger and more sensitive than formerly. This heightens concern about instability in financial markets and the possibility of overshooting, particularly of exchange rates and interest rates. Overshooting may cause resource mis-allocation both because economic agents receive the wrong price signals, and so make the wrong decisions, and because many valuable resources are unnecessarily expended in hedging and speculation. However, much volatility is related to changes in real developments and in expectations about the future, and more efficient markets should keep us closer than otherwise to equilibrium. Furthermore, the possibility of massive capital flows can prevent governments following foolhardy and inconsistent policies. At least, capital flows and exchange rate pressures can provide an efficient early warning, or kind of barometer, of adverse economic conditions ahead, allowing serious problems to be nipped in the bud.

It is also argued that governments may find their room for manœuvre reduced on the fiscal front. At the micro level individual taxes may cause problems and have to be brought into line with what the globalized market will stand—as was the case with the German withholding tax. At the macro level some governments may find that they have to run tighter fiscal policies than they would choose on domestic grounds alone because otherwise massive capital outflows would jeopardize exchange rate policies or drive interest rates to undesirably high levels.

The influence of globalization on fiscal policy appears in different ways under fixed and floating exchange rates. With floating, a money-financed government deficit would lead to depreciation, which could be larger and swifter after globalization with a correspondingly larger inflationary impetus from the tradeable goods sector. The larger exchange rate fall could lead to larger changes in competitiveness, reducing demand and output abroad and perhaps prompting calls for protectionism. Foreign holders of assets denominated in the currency of the expansionary country would suffer exchange rate losses. Thus the policy would have effects beyond the boundaries of the nation pursuing it. Under fixed rates, an individual country could choose to increase its budget deficit, putting upward pressure on interest rates (assuming bond finance) in other countries also. The implication in both cases is that some degree of fiscal co-ordination may be useful. This seems logical if one accepts that there is a link between fiscal position and monetary conditions given the increased need for monetary policy consistency, though the restraint on fiscal autonomy may not be very strong. It is worth noting that the individual states in the USA may adopt different fiscal positions according to their own needs and preferences, and constrained by their respective constitutions, though in fact state budgets vary narrowly around balance.

If today's stronger links between financial economies implies a greater need for co-ordination of fiscal policies at both the micro and macro levels, it seems likely that the market now plays a greater role in achieving this consistency. The advantage of the market's co-ordination is that it is flexible and continuous, for example in allowing differences in relative fiscal position according to differences in private sector financial positions. Therefore globalization may imply a lesser role for formal co-ordination of fiscal policies. Some national authorities may wish to try to stay ahead of the market, on the grounds that if the market forces consistency of policies this may be over a relatively short time scale, possibly in a way that the authorities will not like.

It is sometimes argued that increased globalization may increase the need for improved co-operation and co-ordination of other policies also. Financial capital may flow increasingly towards those

Table 3. Borrowing on international capital markets by main borrowers (% of total)

	1981–4 (average)	1985	1986	1987	1988	1989 January–August
OECD area	70.8	83.3	90.9	89.1	91.2	92.4
Developing countries	22.9	9.2	5.0	6.7	5.0	3.0
Eastern Europe	0.9	1.9	1.0	0.9	1.0	0.8
Others	5.4	5.6	3.1	3.3	2.8	3.8

Note: Figures from 1985 include international equities, euro-commercial paper programmes and other non-underwritten facilities.
Source: OECD.

economies that are the most flexible and productive, and if physical capital relocates to the same economies, existing imbalances in output, production, and income distribution may increase. However, this is not an inevitable result: gross flows of financial capital may gravitate to the most developed financial centres, but, as with Britain in the nineteenth century, this may serve to increase physical investment elsewhere in the world rather than in the financial centre. By enabling investment to be more distant from saving globalization should help, not hinder, investment in LDCs.

There are concerns that as monetary and economic integration increases in the advanced countries, many of the LDCs will be marginalized, and that globalization will facilitate financial flows between the advanced economies and so restrict flows to the LDCs. The statistical evidence (Table 3) shows that flows of financial capital have increasingly focused on OECD countries (particularly the UK, USA, and Japan), with the share accounted for by developing countries having dropped from some 23 per cent in 1981–4 to only 5 per cent last year. However, this relative decline may reflect to a large extent the debt crisis in the developing world rather than globalization.

If the ability of LDCs to come to the globalized market is limited, can the globalized market go to the LDCs? The financial systems of many LDCs may be neither sufficiently developed nor sufficiently robust to compete in a liberalized market, and governments may wish to restrict penetration by foreign financial firms to maintain national control over the financial system. Paradoxically, therefore, globalization, which is based on increasing linkages between economies and financial systems, may in the short run increase some existing divisions.

Over the longer run, however, the increased availability of financial capital represents an opportunity for all potential borrowers. As shown by the global recycling of the oil surpluses in the 1970s (and the experience of some of the faster developing countries today), LDCs are not automatically excluded from global financial development. In the nineteenth century there were substantial capital flows to developing countries, for example to South America. It does not follow, therefore, that globalization will by itself disadvantage the LDCs; it is rather that the current debt problems that many face prevent them from benefiting from it directly. However, fewer distortions in the developed countries should increase output, raising the demand for products from the LDCs and benefiting them indirectly.

4. Where is it leading?

It seems likely that the globalization process will continue, since further liberalization will free capital flows in more countries; because the barriers between banking and securities houses are breaking down; because of continued advances in technology and financial engineering; and because end-users of globalized financial services see further gains to be made. Also, the global financial intermediaries are certain to continue to market and develop more sophisticated products.

Even if some countries lose out as a consequence of globalization (in relative terms and perhaps absolutely), it seems unlikely that this will provoke a reversal of the globalization process (because most countries are benefiting from it) or cause the disadvantaged countries to opt out and go their own way. A complete reversal of globalization would be extremely damaging and disruptive. Corporations and financial intermediaries would be denied sources of finance on which they rely, with profound implications for their investment and output decisions. Governments too would be hit hard. For example, no recourse to foreign financing would mean that aggregate US saving would have to rise relative to investment, implying a severely restrictive fiscal policy. For individual countries to opt out of globalization would be to choose autarky. Historical precedents hardly suggest that this is the route to prosperity, and it is unlikely to be a popular option.

In the light of the analysis above, we can expect that the continuing trend towards globalization will mean: first, a restriction of the degree to which independent monetary policy and control is effective; second, some lessening of fiscal independence; third, possible increased inequality between nations; and fourth, an increased need for economic co-operation and co-ordination.

It is easy to agree that increased co-ordination is a 'good thing', but much more difficult to achieve it in practice. Partly this is because governments will inevitably continue to put the interests of their own nationals first. It will also be difficult to co-ordinate policies because this requires an agreed framework, or model, within which to work. This is not simple for individual economies—as witnessed by the large number of competing economic and econometric models—and achieving agreement on how the world as a whole works will be even more difficult, particularly as globalization changes the underlying economic structure, perhaps in ways that are not easily foreseeable.

The need for detailed formal co-ordination may be overstated, because we are still some way off from a world of perfectly integrated capital markets; considerable room remains for differences in structure and policy. To employ a sporting analogy, for example, in a soccer team it is desirable that there be a degree of co-ordination—that all the team members should be playing in the same direction, that they should not obstruct each other, and so on. But at the same time there is room for individuality and diversity, and teams with a wide spread of differing strengths and complementary skills may be the strongest. Also, one should be careful not to overlook the powerful role that markets play in producing consistent policies in different countries. The further the globalization process proceeds, the greater the market's role in this will be. Since market participants have much more information available to them in aggregate than do governments and central banks, the most effective, continuous, and efficient form of co-ordination over long periods may be by the market. Thus while the world financial 'team' needs to have broadly common aims, the game plan need not be very detailed—a broad and consistent outline will suffice. The main exceptions to this are likely to be when one economy intends a sharp policy change, or where there is a sudden shock to the system—as in October 1987.

Continuing globalization will sometimes lead to difficult decisions, but currently most governments are going with the flow, some enthusiastically, some less willingly. The loss of independence which is to some degree implicit in the process cannot be judged good or bad on purely economic grounds and will be seen less favourably in countries implementing policies different from those elsewhere, since they will be constrained most. To the extent that the structure of global financial interrelationships changes more quickly than other international linkages, there may be strain in the system as a whole, though the financial flows will in many cases herald, and smooth the way for, closer integration in real economies also. Unless this happens it may be that for some countries—those that are slow to adapt—the costs of globalization may exceed benefits, even though the world as a whole gains.

From Baker to Brady: Managing International Debt

THIRD PRIZE

Editors' Introduction

Third Prize winner William Cline of the Institute for International Economics analyses the rather mixed results of the Baker Plan and examines the prospects for the Brady initiative. The author argues that in some respects the Baker Plan did achieve its goals—debt-servicing burdens were reduced and countries which followed sound policies saw their economies grow. However the Plan did not live up to expectations, with the blame being put on the failure of banks to provide new finance. The banks actually came close to meeting their Baker targets, if debt-equity conversion is viewed as equivalent to rolling over principal, whereas the official sector was considerably further off. On the part of the countries themselves, commitment to reform was patchy and growth slow.

The author stresses that the success of the Brady initiative depends on the process remaining voluntary, as mandatory requirements on banks would damage the prospects for future borrowing by the country. With funds available for enhancing debt reduction being limited, new money will continue to be essential to enable countries to meet their debt service obligations. In the wider perspective, however, the author stresses that poor economic performance continues to be primarily a result of poor domestic policies rather than due to excessive external debt.

William R. Cline, 48, is a Senior Fellow at the Institute for International Economics, Washington DC. A graduate of Princeton (1963), he received his MA (1964) and Ph.D. (1969) in economics from Yale University. Before joining the Institute for International Economics, he was a lecturer and assistant professor of economics at Princeton University (1967-70); a Ford Foundation visiting professor in Brazil (1970-1); Deputy Director of Development and Trade Research, office of the Assistant Secretary for International Affairs, US Treasury Department (1971-3); and Senior Fellow, the Brookings Institution (1973-81). Dr Cline has published frequently on issues in international economics, debt, and trade.

5

From Baker to Brady: Managing International Debt

WILLIAM R. CLINE

In October of 1985, US Treasury Secretary James Baker announced a three-year plan for management of the international debt problem. On 10 March 1989 his successor Nicholas Brady announced a reformulation of the strategy. This essay reviews the progress and shortcomings of the Baker Plan and considers the prospects for the Brady Plan.

The Baker Plan, 1986–1988

In the first few months after Mexico suspended payments in mid-1982, there was great fear of widespread defaults and enormous damage to banks and the international financial system. Emergency lending programs averted disaster, and by 1984 global economic recovery and ebbing interest rates gave hope that the problem was on its way to resolution. But by 1985 policy-makers in Latin America were increasingly frustrated by the recessionary adjustments their countries had been forced to make, led by sharp cutbacks in imports, and by growing evidence that voluntary bank-lending was not likely to return soon. Mexico faced increasing difficulties as oil prices eased, and a devastating earthquake dealt a physical and psychological blow. The activist Baker Treasury decided to move.

The Plan—The Baker Plan sought to strengthen the debt-management strategy through emphasis on long-term growth, in contrast to the often contractionary short-term stabilization programs of the first two years of the debt crisis. Private banks were to extend new credits of $7 billion annually to fifteen large debtor nations, equal to $2\frac{1}{2}$ per cent annual growth in their claims. The debtor countries were to undertake structural reform: trade liberalization, slimming down of the state sector, and liberalization of foreign investment. The multilateral development banks (MDBs) were to increase net disbursements by \$3 billion annually over three years, to the same \$7 billion annual target set for the banks (for a considerable rise in the public-sector share of lending).

All parties knew that the global economy would have to be healthy for the plan to work. A return to interest rates in the high teens or to world-wide recession would ruin the chances for even well-run debtor economies to grow out of the debt crisis through increased exports. Fortunately, the world economy delivered. Growth averaged 3.3 per cent annually in the industrial countries from 1986 through 1988, and LIBOR averaged 7.3 per cent. Although commodity prices were weak in 1986–7, by 1988 they had surged back to levels not seen since the beginning of the decade. The one major disappointment was in oil prices, which fell by more than half in 1986. Oil is more important for exporters (Mexico, Venezuela) than for importers (Brazil, Chile), so the collapse of oil prices was a serious blow to the Baker Plan.

There were some doubts that the Plan would suffice even with good luck. The sudden cutoff of new lending had meant a swing of some \$40 billion in the annual transfer of resources to the debtor countries. The Baker target of \$10 billion annually would redress only one-fourth of the cutback. A more adequate capital flow target would have been closer to \$20 billion annually.

Progress on debt—From the narrow standpoint of external debt management, the Baker period witnessed more progress than is generally recognized. The best measure of the external debt burden is the ratio of interest to exports of goods and services. This measure showed major improvement in the key Latin American debtor countries. From its peak year (typically in 1982 or 1983) to 1988, the interest/exports ratio fell from 57 per cent to 30 per cent in Brazil, 47 per cent to 29 per cent in Mexico, 58 per cent to 40 per cent in Argentina, 31 per cent to 26 per cent in Venezuela, 50 per cent to 23 per cent in Chile, and 27 per cent to 21 per cent in Colombia.[1] For Latin America as a whole, the ratio declined from 41 per cent in 1982 to 28 per cent by 1988, returning to its level in 1981 before the debt crisis.

Growth and inflation—There were few cheers for the improvement in the traditional credit-worthiness indicators for the key Latin American debtors. Instead, policy-makers in debtor countries cited, and the public sensed, deterioration in the bottom line: inflation and growth. On these criteria 1988 was one of the worst years on record, as growth in Latin America averaged only 0.7 per cent, and inflation 473 per cent. Nor were creditors much encouraged. Their attention focused on yet another indicator: the secondary market price of bank claims. The (weighted) average price of debt for twenty-four debtor countries had fallen from almost 70 cents on the dollar at the beginning of the Baker Plan period to about 35 cents at its end.[2]

Bank lending—In the popular view, the principal failure of the Baker Plan was that the banks did not meet their lending targets. The inference might be that low growth in Latin America was the consequence of inadequate capital flows, and that the banks were to blame. The record is somewhat different.

BIS (Bank for International Settlements) data indicate that from the end of 1985 to end-1988, the claims of industrial country banks on the fifteen Baker Plan countries[3] fell by $9.7 billion in contrast to the Baker Plan target of a $20 billion increase.[4] However, during this period the banks also carried out $26 billion in debt conversion and reduction for the Baker 15 countries. They converted some $15.5 billion into equity or local currency, $1 billion into exit bonds, eliminated $1 billion through buybacks, and reduced debt by $8 billion in discounted restructurings.[5] These reductions were not business-as-usual amortizations (which would appropriately be deducted from new lending), but instead amounted to strengthening the debt-management process.[6] If these amounts are added into the BIS totals, the effective expansion of exposure *cum* debt reduction amounted to $16 billion, or four-fifths of the Baker target.

Another measure of bank lending performance was the total of new-money packages over the Baker Plan period. During 1986–88, the banks disbursed $12.8 billion in concerted lending.[7] As little amortization was taking place, the new-money packages provided a relatively good guide to net new lending. On this criterion, the banks met approximately 60 per cent of their Baker Plan lending target. In short, measures more meaningful than the raw data on outstanding exposure suggest that the banks went relatively far in fulfilling their task under the Baker Plan.[8]

Public-sector lending—For its part, the official sector delivered only a relatively small share of the intended increase in lending under the Baker Plan. Average net disbursements of the multilateral development banks to the Baker countries rose from $3.86 billion

annually in 1983–5 to \$4.2 billion annually in 1986–8.[9] The
increment thus amounted to only one-tenth of the intended \$3
billion annually. Moreover, if the IMF is included the results were
far worse. In 1986–8, the IMF made net withdrawals averaging
\$900 million annually from the Baker-fifteen countries (with eleven
of the fifteen showing net transfers to the institution). In contrast,
in 1983 the IMF had contributed net inflows of approximately \$6
billion to these countries.[10] Including the IMF and bilateral export
credit agencies together with the MDBs, net official disbursements
to the Baker-fifteen declined from \$9 billion annually in 1983–5 to
only \$5 billion annually in 1986–8. The Baker Plan's failure to set
a lending target for the entire official community including the IMF
(and thereby to provide for larger goals for multilateral bank
lending to compensate for expected declines in IMF lending) was
one of its principal shortcomings.

Country performance—Some of the debtor countries made good
on their commitment to structural reform under the Baker Plan.

Mexico went the furthest. In 1986 Mexico joined the GATT. By
early 1988 its maximum tariff was down to 20 per cent and its
average tariff 10 per cent, and less than one-fourth of imports
remained subject to licensing. Mexico's fiscal adjustment was
remarkable, as the government cut non-interest spending by 10 per
cent of GNP. The government privatized a large copper company
and a major airline, and in 1989 the new Salinas regime liberalized
regulations on foreign ownership. Macro economic management
none-the-less remained disappointing in many countries, particularly
in Argentina and Brazil (and worse, Peru). Failure to reach
agreement on IMF standby programs was one of the main reasons
for limited lending from the international institutions and the banks.

External Debt, Growth, and Stability

Macro-performance and the debt burden—By the end of the Baker
Plan period, external debt was widely blamed for low growth and
high inflation. However, the evidence suggests that those countries
that pursued appropriate domestic policies were able to achieve
relatively favourable growth and moderate inflation, and that the
external-debt burden was not the primary cause of explosive
inflation and slow growth elsewhere in the region. Thus, in the
1986–88 period, the six largest Latin American debtor countries

divided into two divergent groups. Chile, Colombia, and Venezuela achieved average growth of 5.2 per cent annually and average inflation of 23 per cent.[11] In contrast, Argentina, Brazil, and Mexico experienced average growth of only 1.9 per cent annually and average inflation of 735 per cent. Yet the burden of debt was actually higher in the first group, which made higher outward resource transfers (averaging 4.6 per cent of GNP) than did the second group (3.6 per cent).[12] The simplest explanation was that domestic macro destabilization, rather than external debt, was primarily responsible for poor growth performance in several major Latin American countries during the Baker Plan period.

The case of Brazil illustrated the dominant weight of domestic policy as opposed to external debt in explaining poor results on growth and inflation. It was apparent that Brazil's broad export base made the 'external transfer' required to service-debt manageable. Indeed, its $19 billion trade surplus in 1988 was the third largest in the world. Some argued that precisely this outward resource transfer was the cause of slow growth, because resources were being diverted abroad that instead could have been used for investment at home. But the plunge of Brazilian growth from a range of some 7 per cent annually to zero could not be explained by the magnitude of the outward transfer. At 4 per cent of GNP (1986–8 average), even if the outward resource transfer[13] were completely eliminated Brazil's growth would rise by only $1\frac{1}{3}$ per cent annually (applying a capital / output ratio of 3), or only a small fraction of the decline in growth that had occurred in the face of 1,000 per cent domestic inflation.

The internal transfer—Increasingly the argument was that external debt was slowing growth not primarily because of its requirement of achieving an external transfer, but because it necessitated the mobilization of an internal transfer from the private sector to the public sector in a situation in which the government was already close to fiscal bankruptcy. For the six largest Latin American debtor countries, government interest payments on external debt rose from $1\frac{1}{2}$ per cent of GNP in 1980–1 to $2\frac{1}{2}$ per cent in 1982–3 and 4 per cent in 1986–7.[14] Moreover, the closure of the external capital market forced governments to borrow more domestically, where real interest rates were typically much higher.

None the less, the real solution to the fiscal problem was much more likely to lie in domestic policies rather than external-debt forgiveness. For example, Brazilian spending on public administration at all levels of government rose by 2.2 percentage points of GDP from 1984 to 1988 as the new civilian regime indulged in a wave of patronage hiring.[15] In contrast, Brazilian public outlays on interest on foreign debt had risen by only about $\frac{1}{2}$ per cent of GNP (from 1981 to their peak in 1985). Similarly, Argentina regularly lost 1 per cent of GNP in deficits of the state railway.

Possible external debt forgiveness as a solution to the domestic fiscal problem raised thorny issues, moreover. From one standpoint, the implied debt reductions could be limited. Government spending in Latin America is typically some 40 per cent of GNP, and the real fiscal deficit in the range of 4 per cent of GNP. The deficit could be eliminated by a spending cut of 10 per cent. If spending on foreign interest payments was treated like all other spending, forgiveness would amount to only one-tenth.

Alternatively, if school lunches and dams are considered more vital than interest payments, the issue would transform into the question of why foreign creditors of the government should forgive if domestic creditors are not asked to do so. Thus, in 1988 Mexico's outlays on real interest on domestic public debt were twice as large as on external debt.[16] Yet Mexican policy-makers were not calling for forgiveness on their domestic debt despite their urging of debt reduction by foreign creditors.

In sum, the fiscal problem lay at the root of macroeconomic destabilization in Latin America, and an increase in interest payments on foreign debt had contributed to fiscal difficulties. Yet it was by no means clear that the correct policy conclusion was the need for foreign-debt forgiveness. In contrast, the fiscal problem did imply there would be major benefits if countries could obtain increased access to foreign capital markets at international interest rates, initially through improved concerted lending but eventually through renewed voluntary lending.

Voluntary Debt Reduction

By the end of the Baker Plan period there was great pressure for moving further in the international debt management strategy. The case against mandatory debt forgiveness remained strong. Latin America had defaulted in the 1930s and been locked out of the capital markets for three to four decades. A repeat of this experience today would be more costly for the region, now that the easy phase of import substitution is past, because an inevitable result would be isolation of debtor countries from international trade and financial markets. It is difficult to conceive of rapid export growth in a country that has become a pariah to the banks, as normal financial channels used by importers abroad would be impaired. The model of export-led growth would be crushed just as policymakers had learned its lessons and begun to pursue it.

A natural opportunity for further action presented itself, however, as the result of the low prices of developing country debt in the secondary markets. The large discounts represented a rent that could be mobilized and shared between creditors and debtor countries on a market-oriented, voluntary basis. Whereas mandated debt reduction would damage the willingness of banks to deal with the country for years to come, no one in the banking community could object if those banks most anxious to exit from lending chose to do so at a discount; indeed, their exit would improve the prospects that the claims of the remaining banks would be honoured, by reducing the debt burden.

Two concepts of voluntary debt reduction have emerged. One postulates that there is a 'debt overhang' that acts like a prohibitive tax on debtor country effort; benefits from increased exports and investment are so disproportionately channelled to debt service, in this view, that government adjustment and investment by firms is far below potential. In short, the notion is that there is a 'Laffer curve for debt'.[17] The horizontal axis shows total nominal debt; the vertical axis, the expected value of the debt to the creditors. The curve starts out along the 45 degree line but then falls below it and, at some critical turning-point, turns down again. If the country is on the wrong side of this turning-point, both the country and the creditors will be better off if the creditors forgive debt down to that point.

This first concept of voluntary debt reduction implies uniform forgiveness by all creditors of a given country. The government or an international agency would identify the debt turning-point, and all banks would then take collective action in their own interests to forgive down to this point. However, there is little reason to think that the major debtors are on the wrong side of a debt Laffer curve. Countries such as Brazil and Chile have shown a strong capacity to expand exports, and the declining interest / export ratios cited above cast doubt on the Laffer curve argument. Indeed, when properly interpreted, statistical equations explaining secondary market prices show that only for a handful of extremely heavily indebted countries would the creditor's expected value of debt rise as the result of debt reduction.[18]

The second concept of debt reduction is much more realistic. It is premised on the existence of two classes of banks: those that intend to remain in Latin America over the next several decades, and those (typically smaller, later-entry banks) that would be happy to exit at 50 cents on the dollar (for example) if they could receive the 50 cents in cash or in highly secure instruments.[19] The natural role for the public sector is then to provide guarantees that permit the creation of these secure instruments and thereby mobilize the potential secondary market rent in favour of the debtor country. In 1988 the banks had already experimented with 'exit bonds' with modest success in the new-money package for Brazil and in the Mexico–Morgan Guaranty conversion of bank claims into long-term bonds secured by zero-coupon Treasury bonds. With official support, the potential for such mechanisms would be much greater.

The Brady Plan

Secretary Brady recognized this opportunity and sought to grasp it. His plan was a key political breakthrough. It broke the shibboleth that the public sector could not provide guarantees for debt reduction because to do so would be 'bailing out the banks', always a curious argument considering that the only banks involved would be those that accepted sizeable forgiveness up front.

The Brady Plan was less concrete in its targets than the Baker Plan. Its essence was to shift the thrust of official policy toward encouragement of voluntary debt reduction. By explicitly referring to voluntary reduction, the plan continued the basic market-related strategy that had existed since the outbreak of the debt crisis. The new approach continued to judge the long-term costs of rupture with financial markets too high relative to any short-term gains to warrant a fundamental shift in policy toward mandated forgiveness.

The closest the plan came to explicit formulation was in testimony by US Treasury Undersecretary David Mulford, who indicated that it could cut the bank debt of some thirty-nine countries by $70 billion (of a total of $340 billion), with proportionately larger cuts possible in countries such as Mexico.[20] Within three months of the plan's announcement, the official community had identified approximately $34 billion in resources to support the plan. The IMF and World Bank were both to set aside approximately one-fourth of policy-based lending for the purpose of principal reduction (or enhancement), for $12 billion over three years. After initial opposition of some European governments, the IMF was further authorized to permit up to 40 per cent of country quota to be used for the securing of interest payments on debt-reduction instruments,[21] with comparable support from the World Bank for a total of an additional $12 billion over three years. And the Japanese government announced that it would provide some $10 billion to support debt reduction (a policy the Japanese had been in the lead in advocating).

In broad terms the plan appeared feasible. The target of $70 billion debt reduction could plausibly be achieved with the $34 billion in public resources available for enhancement. The Mexico–Morgan exercise had shown that leveraging of $1 in guarantee resources to back $5 in face value of conversion bonds was too thin; the market had been unwilling to offer a discount of more than 30 cents on the dollar, whereas at the going secondary market price it would have offered up to 50 cents if the instrument had been considered secure. The missing ingredient was a guarantee on interest, as the collateral on distant principal was of limited value.

Leveraging of 1 to 1 would probably be unnecessarily rich, however. Especially with the umbrella effect of participation of the IMF and World Bank (against whom countries are extremely reluctant to default), it is likely that $1 in official resources could back $2 in exit bond instruments. If the average forgiveness in the plan were 50 cents on the dollar, then the target of $70 billion debt reduction would correspond to conversion of an initial $140 billion in claims to only $70 billion.[22] The pool of $34 billion in official resources could plausibly back $70 billion in converted debt.

More specifically, an appropriate instrument could be as follows. Zero-coupon bonds could be used to collateralize principal on thirty-year bonds, at a cost of approximately 10 cents for each dollar to be backed. In addition, four years' rolling interest guarantee could be provided for approximately another 40 cents.

The total resources required to back each dollar face value of the exit bond would thus amount to 50 cents.

It would be desirable if the Brady Plan could expand to a target closer to $50 billion for public resources to back debt reduction. Some $100 billion of conversion bonds could then be backed, permitting a reduction in debt by perhaps $100 billion rather than $70 billion.

Public pronouncements on the Brady Plan were careful to note that new money would still be required from the banking community. Thus, if out of $340 billion bank claims, $140 billion were reduced to $70 billion, the other $200 billion would remain intact and banks holding the unchanged claims would need to participate in new-money packages to help finance some of the interest coming due.

The banks sought new enhancements to facilitate new money. One option was a carefully circumscribed form of World Bank co-financing, in which the institution would be committed to share receipts on a co-financed loan if the country did not pay the banks, but only on that loan and with no impact on the rest of the World Bank's portfolio on the country. Another helpful measure would be for regulators to waive loan-loss reserves on new money in internationally approved adjustment packages. But fundamentally the incentive to provide new money remained the same as for the past six years: by modest new lending the banks could shore up their large outstanding stakes.[23] Moreover, with smaller actors taken out by enhanced exit bonds, the mechanics of concerted lending among the remaining banks were likely to improve.

These were the potential carrots. The Brady Plan also included a stick. It shifted IMF policy to permit 'lending into arrears'. In the past the IMF had tended to tell countries they needed to work out an arrangement with banks on arrears before IMF resources could be loaned. Policy-makers were sensitive to the charge that the IMF was becoming the 'policeman of the banks', and in some cases (such as that of Costa Rica) some felt that reasonable country programs were not winning the appropriate support of the banks. The new policy meant that if the country had a good economic program, the IMF and World Bank would lend (and, as a side benefit, thereby ensure that the country would not go into arrears against them) even if the banks had not agreed to a financial package.[24]

At mid-1989 the key test case for the Brady Plan was Mexico. Negotiators for that country presented an IMF-approved proposal to the banks calling for some $3 billion to $4½ billion in annual financial support, ideally through the forgiveness of 55 per cent of the $53 billion in medium-term claims but alternatively through new money or interest capitalization amounting to 80 per cent of interest due. The banks argued that the request was too ambitious, and questioned the economic assumptions (for example, on oil prices) in the program.[25]

The Mexican case immediately illustrated a central dilemma in the Brady Plan. The more the official sector leaned on the banks to deliver a target amount of forgiveness, the less voluntary the process remained and the more potential damage to long-term capital market relationships there might be—including for third parties (such as Thailand) who might be adversely affected if the perception grew that international lending was inevitably subject to forgiveness imposed by the public sector. Statements by Under-secretary Mulford (that the banks might face legislated forgiveness if they did not co-operate) and IMF Managing Director Camdessus (reported in the press as 'blaming the banks' for slow progress under the Brady Plan) illustrated the tension between a plan conceived of as market-oriented and voluntary on the one hand, and official-sector notions of what was required on the other.[26]

Essentially all parties had to decide whether debt reduction was to be a positive-sum game, or whether it was going to slide into a zero- or negative-sum game with the official sector mandating a transfer from creditors to debtors. In the latter case, policy-makers would have to make the complicated and uncertain calculation of the trade-off between immediate relief and longer-term adverse effects for the debtor country itself. Nor was the issue solely one of adequate public guarantees. There was strong evidence that many large banks considered Mexico to have the potential to honour far closer to 90 or 100 cents on the dollar over time than only 45 cents, and these banks would not be likely to grant 55 per cent forgiveness even if offered the remainder in cold cash.

It was correspondingly important that debtor-country negotiators and the official sector keep in mind the dual nature of the banking community and voluntary debt relief. It would be mistaken to seek uniform forgiveness by all banks; across-the-board debt reduction would either be minimal or would require mandatory action.

Three months after announcement of the Brady Plan, it seemed likely that Mexico, the banks, and the international official community would come to a bargain that provided significant debt reduction and new money (with the greater part probably new money).[27] Realism and continued attention to longer-term effects would be required on all sides. As before, the Brady Plan could only work if the international economic environment was not adverse. Economic policies in the industrial countries were thus crucial. The failure of the United States to make a convincing attack on its large fiscal deficit had boosted LIBOR to approximately $10\frac{1}{2}$ per cent even as Secretary Brady announced his plan. If sustained, the rise of 300 basis points from the 1986–8 average would cost the debtor countries $11 billion annually on their bank debt, more than offsetting the $7 billion annual interest savings they stood to gain from a reduction of $70 billion debt under the plan.

Fortunately, the debtor countries, the banks, and policy-makers in industrial countries have consistently shown the pragmatism to adjust their approach to international debt and avert a breakdown. The Brady Plan is a welcome step in the evolution of international debt policy. If implemented with astuteness and understanding of the economics underlying voluntary debt reduction, and especially if expanded through additional resources, the Plan holds promise for facilitating economic recovery and reviving political hope in debtor countries.

Postscript

Approximately one month after the submission deadline for this essay, in late July, Mexican negotiators reached agreement with the banks on the first debt-reduction programme under the Brady Plan. As predicted above, both sides agreed to a realistic compromise. The banks met Mexico two-thirds of the way by pledging to reduce debt by 35 per cent, cut interest rates to 6.25 per cent annually, or extend new loans amounting to 60 per cent of interest coming due over the next four years. The principal and interest-reduction bonds were to be collateralized with thirty-year US Treasury zero coupon bonds for principal, with eighteen months guarantee on interest.

The favourable impact of the agreement on confidence within Mexico turned out to be dramatic. The annual real interest rate on government obligations fell from 33 per cent to 14 per cent, saving some $10 billion (6 per cent of GNP) in annual budget costs. Although leftist groups in Mexico, and some US academics, assailed the agreement as inadequate, its annual cash-flow benefits were within $600 million of the amount originally requested,[28] a sufficiently small divergence (2 per cent of exports of goods and services) to be within the range of error in balance-of-payments forecasts, and less than one-tenth of the fiscal gains from lower domestic interest rates.

International reactions were revealing. Soon after the Mexico agreement, the Philippines struck a deal with the banks that involved new money but no uniform formula for debt reduction; instead, the government planned to re-purchase debt at a discount from the secondary market. Philippine planners sought a more market-oriented approach with less arm-twisting of the banks than in the Mexican case, because they hoped for early return to the capital market. For the same reason, the Colombian government announced that it would not seek a Mexico-type package. And although initially Venezuelan negotiators insisted that they would seek 50 per cent debt reduction despite the Mexican example, within two months they had de-escalated their demands and were pursuing a more flexible approach, relating the depth of debt reduction to the degree of security of the converted debt. In short, policy-makers in several key debtor countries seemed to be concluding that it was worth accepting debt relief less than or equal to that adopted by Mexico, to avoid a severe break in relations with banks that could result from insistence on far deeper discounts. Because the IMF (and by implication the US government) had signed off on Mexico's more ambitious initial request of 55 per cent debt reduction, debtor-country governments (including that of Mexico) were in the unusual position of being more pragmatic than Northern policy-makers.

The other principal development was a new wave of concern that the banks would cut and run, getting a 'cheap ride' of total exit at 35 cents loss on the dollar. Morgan, Chase, and Manufacturers' Hanover set aside large additional reserves, raising the spectre of mass exodus. US officials, including the President, found themselves pressing the banks to continue lending some new money, a renewed emphasis that there were two tracks to the Brady Plan after all, and that while some banks should choose debt reduction, others should choose new money (as argued above).[29] Curiously, after having seemed to threaten banks with adverse legislation if they did not forgive debt, now some high US officials seemed to be threatening the same punishment if too many banks chose debt forgiveness rather than new money.[30] Such was the schizophrenia that remained in the regime transition from the Baker Plan to the Brady Plan.

Part of the problem was the rigid formulation of the Mexican agreement. Instead of a single depth of reduction of 35 per cent (with minor variation between the principal and interest alternatives), it would have been possible to offer both a more highly secured but more deeply discounted 'gold-plated' exit bond (for example, with 50 per cent reduction and 6 years' interest guarantee), and an instrument with the 35 per cent discount but less security (for example, only one year's interest guarantee). This differentiation would have been more likely to separate the banks into the two groupings discussed above (exit-oriented and long-horizon), and achieve the same aggregate debt reduction while leaving a larger group of banks in the new-money option and thus committed to Mexico's future. The ultimate form of this differentiation is to include discounted buybacks, which provide the deepest discount (i.e. the secondary market rate) and the highest security (cold cash).

A related emerging obstacle to new money was the continuing trend of regulators in the United Kingdom, continental Europe, and Canada to require high loan-loss reserves (50 per cent or more) on both old and new money. Yet the logic of a Brady package was that the country would be able to honour the obligations that remained. US regulators argued for exempting such new lending from reserves, but official positions abroad appeared entrenched.

Despite these difficulties and the signs that all parties were still feeling their way, the Brady Plan was off to a good start with the Mexico package. The next step was to extend the Plan to other debtor countries, including the important cases of Venezuela, Argentina (if the new President Carlos Menem delivered on his programme of forceful economic restructuring), and, if warranted after changed policies by a new President in 1990, Brazil. It would take perhaps a year before the early returns would begin to come in on the central question of whether, this time, the revised international debt strategy would be adequate.

Notes

1. ECLA, *Preliminary Overview of the Latin American Economy 1988*. Referred to below as *ECLA 1988*.
2. Salomon Brothers.
3. Argentina, Bolivia, Brazil, Chile, Colombia, Ecuador, Ivory Coast, Mexico, Morocco, Nigeria, Peru, Philippines, Uruguay, Venezuela, Yugoslavia.
4. Bank for International Settlements, *Statistics on External Indebtedness* (Basle, July 1986); *International Banking and Financial Market Development* (Basle, May 1989). Note that cumulative exchange-rate valuation changes in the debt were close to zero over this period.
5. Institute of International Finance, *The Way Forward for Middle-Income Countries* (Washington, IIF, January 1989), p. 22.
6. The intense controversy over debt-equity conversions, and in particular their potential inflationary consequences, will not be examined here. For purposes of assessing bank-lending performance, conversion into equity surely was equivalent to rolling over principal, and indeed more advantageous to debtor countries to the extent that they received discounts. Yet debt-equity conversion shows up in the data as a reduction in principal, thereby understating the net expansion of bank claims.
7. World Bank, *World Debt Tables 1988-89 Edition*, vol. I, p. xxliii. Referred to below as *World Debt Tables 1988*. The figure here deducts $1.96 billion for Colombia (rollover of principal rather than new money) and adds $4 billion for Brazil in late 1988.
8. The one area where there was a clear shortfall was for the smaller countries, many not even included in the Baker group. The fixed costs of interbank arm-twisting in concerted lending were apparently high relative to potential bank benefits from lending packages to the smaller countries because the stakes were limited.
9. Calculated from World Bank, *World Debt Tables 1988*, vol. II and by communication.
10. IMF *International Financial Statistics*, various issues; World Bank, *World Development Tables 1988*, vol. I, p. 30.
11. Albeit with the aid of distorting price controls in the case of Venezuela.
12. Calculated from *ECLA 1988* and *International Financial Statistics*.
13. Measured as the difference between net interest and profits payments and net inflows of capital, from *ECLA 1988*.
14. Calculated from *World Debt Tables 1988*, vol. II.
15. *Veja*, 15 March 1989, p. 84.
16. Banco de Mexico, *Informe Anual 1988*.
17. See, for example, Paul Krugman, 'Market-based Debt-Reduction Schemes', NBER Working Paper no. 2587 (May 1988).

¹⁸ Thus, Sachs and Huizinga estimate an equation that shows the secondary market price as a negative linear function of the debt / GNP ratio. Although the authors do not note this point, this price equation may be multiplied by the level of debt to obtain the expected value of debt to the creditors. The first derivative of this value with respect to the debt / GNP ratio turns negative only after debt exceeds 180 to 270 per cent of GNP, far in excess of levels observed in major debtor countries. Jeffrey Sachs and Harry Huizinga, 'US Commercial Banks and the Developing-Country Debt Crisis', *Brookings Papers on Economic Activity* 2 (1987), pp. 555–606.

¹⁹ William R. Cline, 'International Debt: Progress and Strategy', *Finance and Development* (June 1988), 9–11; John Williamson, *Voluntary Approaches to Debt Relief* (Washington: Institute for International Economics, September 1988). Note that prudential limits (not to mention critical comment from bank-stock analysts) prevent the first group of banks from buying up the debt from the second.

²⁰ *Washington Post*, 17 March 1989.

²¹ Note that the decision to link interest support funds to IMF quotas was questionable, because quotas had little relationship to country shares in debt to commercial banks.

²² This illustration assumes that the cut is made in principal. It could also be made by reducing interest on unchanged principal with little difference in the economics of required backing. Also note that for countries with extremely low secondary-market prices, it could be more attractive to use Brady Plan resources primarily for discounted debt buybacks.

²³ The calculus of new money is as follows: banks will lend more so long as the resulting reduction in probability of default, multiplied by the existing debt (the expected benefit of the new money), exceeds the terminal probability of default, multiplied by the amount of new lending (its expected cost).

²⁴ The club in the closet went further: countries could legitimate such situations by invoking Article 8.2.B of the IMF articles of agreement, which authorizes governments to impose exchange controls limiting debt service-payments in foreign currency.

²⁵ The $4½ billion in annual financing (if all banks choose the option of relending 80 per cent of interest) was close to what might be called the 'Ponzi point' of re-lending the entirety of interest.

²⁶ *Washington Post*, 25 May and 1 June 1989.

²⁷ Only about $6 billion in official funds for debt enhancement had been mobilized for Mexico, plus another $1 billion from Mexico's reserves. Assuming the 2-to-1 leverage outlined above, these funds could back $14 billion in conversion bonds. With 50 cents forgiven on the dollar

in these bonds, $28 billion in original debt would be cut to $14 billion. The interest savings would amount to $1.4 billion annually, or less than half of effective financing even if the target were scaled down to $3 billion annually. The rest would have to come from new money. (Author's note: as discussed below, in the event, the banks turned out to be more willing to accept exit instruments with considerably less than 50 per cent backing.)

[28] At the government's expected mix of 20 per cent new money, 60 per cent interest reduction, and 20 per cent debt reduction, the package would save $1.6 billion in annual interest and provide $2.3 billion in annual cash flow. If all banks had forgiven 55 per cent, the interest and cash-flow benefits would have been $2.9 billion annually.

[29] The proximate concern was that unless banks with at least 20 per cent of claims opted for new money, the Mexico package would collapse because of too little cash flow and too great a requirement for enhancements. In fact this risk was not acute, in part because foreign branches of Mexican banks alone accounted for about 10 per cent of the debt and were automatically in the new-money group. In addition, there were emerging hints that Mexican officials, who sought at least one major bank in each major country to stay in the new-money option, would channel future financial sector business the way of co-operating banks.

[30] Paul Blustein, 'US Official Presses Banks to Make Loans to Mexico', *Washington Post*, 6 October 1989.

Domestic Deficits, Debt Overhang, and Capital Outflows in Developing Countries

SPECIAL MERIT AWARD

Editors' Introduction

Using empirical evidence of the magnitude of capital flight from debtor countries in the 1980s, Przemyslaw Gajdeczka and Daniel Oks of the IMF and World Bank (respectively) look for satisfactory explanations of this phenomenon. The essay argues that the nature of capital flight pre-1982 can be explained by poor domestic policies resulting in adverse economic incentives for domestic investors and facilitated by large inflows from foreign creditors. The authors then search for an explanation for the resurgence in capital flight since 1986, and argue that debtor governments not only lost external credit-worthiness (in 1982–3) but have now also lost domestic credit-worthiness. As confidence in governments has been eroded, the perceived risk of domestic assets has risen and residents have sought to diversify through investing abroad. While this continues still at the core of the problem of capital flight today, the authors also look at several other explanations of the problem, for example continuing policy distortions, 'debt overhang', and uncertainty over debt negotiations.

Przemyslaw T. Gajdeczka, 36, is a Polish national, permanently resident in the United States. He received his Masters and Doctoral degrees in economics from the Central School of Planning and Statistics in Warsaw. Now working at the Current Studies Division in the Research Department of the International Monetary Fund, he spent two years in the World Bank as analyst and editor of a quarterly publication monitoring resource flows to developing countries. Before the World Bank, he worked as economist for the Centrally Planned Economies Service of Wharton Econometrics, a US forecasting and consulting firm. His areas of research interest include external debt issues, international capital flows, and debt and finance developments in Eastern Europe.

Daniel F. Oks, 36, is an Argentine national. After graduating from Buenos Aires University he obtained a Master's degree at the London School of Economics and a D.Phil. in Economics at Oxford University. Dr Oks did research and taught at Buenos Aires University and worked at the First National Bank of Boston in Argentina. Currently he is an economist at the Debt and International Finance Division of the World Bank. His areas of research interest include fiscal and monetary policy in developing countries and external debt and finance issues in Latin America.

6

Domestic Deficits, Debt Overhang, and Capital Outflows in Developing Countries

PRZEMYSLAW GAJDECZKA AND DANIEL OKS*

1. Introduction

Large capital flows out of developing countries have provided ample evidence of high capital mobility between LDCs and the outside world and of private capital's strong responsiveness to changes in both domestic and foreign economic incentives. Because LDC governments largely ignored capital mobility and allowed policy distortions to persist, capital flight continued until external credit was denied and some corrective measures were undertaken. However, the price LDCs paid for capital flight was already high.

Although massive foreign lending has played an instrumental role in facilitating private capital outflows, the deeper roots of capital flight can be traced back to the economic disincentives created by domestic policy distortions. In particular, large public-sector deficits, exchange rate overvaluation, and financial instability raised the risks associated with domestic investment. Economic uncertainty in Highly Indebted Countries (HICs) was further aggravated by the external debt burden which, in turn, was largely a consequence of policy distortions. The decline in outflows from the early 1980s through 1986 can be ascribed in part to the correction of some distortions, such as the reduction in exchange-rate overvaluation, the decline in the non-financial portion of government deficits and the drying-up of foreign credit.

* Both authors were economists in the Debt and International Finance Division of the World Bank at the time of writing the paper. Dr. Gajdeczka is now with the International Monetary Fund. However, the views expressed in this paper are those of the authors only and do not necessarily reflect the position of the World Bank or the IMF. The authors acknowledge to have benefited from a growing body of literature on external debt and capital flight, although no specific references are made in this paper. The detailed discussion of capital flight estimates and the underlying methodology was presented by one of the authors in 'Financial Flows in Developing Countries', *Quarterly Review, World Bank* (March 1989).

The revival of capital flight after 1986, however, requires new explanations. One is the loss of credit-worthiness of indebted developing countries. The deterioration of governments' credit-worthiness raised the risk premium on domestic investments and, in that context, capital flight became a mechanism for arbitraging out differentials between risk-adjusted domestic and foreign rates of return. Another explanation for the recent resurgence of capital flight is related to the 'internal transfer' problem. The internal transfer refers to the transfer of resources from the private to the public sector in order to finance current government expenditures. During the 1980s, the internal transfer has risen in magnitude due to the increase in foreign debt service and, more recently, due to the explosive growth in domestic public debt service. As the internal transfer problem intensified it fostered capital flight because of the looming tax liability which posed a threat to domestic held wealth.

The third explanation is based on the 'debt overhang' argument, which states that large foreign public debt discourages domestic investment because of fears that taxes will rise in the future to service the foreign debt. This concern is an obvious incentive for capital flight. Whereas the internal transfer poses a threat to both present domestic wealth and income, the debt overhang argument points to disincentive effects of future additional income taxation.

A fourth explanation for capital flight stresses the role of uncertainty. The large foreign public debt is a source of instability and uncertainty because the outcome of debtor–creditor negotiations is difficult to predict and the fiscal burden of the foreign debt accentuates the political struggle for scarce fiscal resources.

The paper is organized as follows. In Section 2 we provide the background for our analysis and we report estimates of capital outflows from debtor countries in recent years. In Section 3 we illustrate the linkages between capital outflows and net foreign lending and, in Section 4 we assess the role of domestic policy distortions in the process of capital flight. We examine the linkages between the internal transfer problem and capital flight in Section 5. In Section 6 we evaluate the impact of international portfolio diversification and increasing LDC involvement in international activity on capital flight. In Section 7 we evaluate the debt overhang and uncertainty hypotheses. Conclusions and policy recommendations are summarized in Section 8.

2. Capital Flight: Magnitude and Importance

Large capital flows out of developing countries have provided evidence of a significant degree of capital mobility in these countries and of the strong responsiveness of capital to changes in economic incentives. Interest in the capital flight problem gradually evolved from the effect it had on external debt, to the potential use of foreign-held assets for reduction of developing country debt. To provide the basis for further discussion of these issues we proceed to review recent trends in capital outflows and assess their importance.

Contrary to the common view, which differentiates between capital flight and other business related capital outflows, we believe that any resident capital that leaves a country does so for economic reasons in response to market incentives, and that this act has balance of payments consequences that provide the basis for our estimates.

Therefore, our measure of capital flight—the 'total outflow' measure—aggregates acquisition of external assets of all sectors of the debtor country (excluding official reserves) recorded in the balance of payments, plus errors and omissions, assumed here to measure unrecorded capital outflows. This measure represents the upper bound on alternative measures of capital flight. However, the effects of trade misinvoicing and transfers hidden in inter-company financial flows of multinational enterprises are most likely not fully, if at all, captured by this measure.

According to our estimates (see Table 1), total capital outflows from the seventeen HICs amounted to nearly $84 billion from 1980 to 1987. Over $51 billion was accounted for by the acquisition of foreign assets (excluding official reserves) by all domestic sectors and the rest remained unidentified as errors and omissions. Despite the resurgence since 1986, capital outflows in recent years showed a significant decline in volume. Recent capital outflows originated mainly from the non-bank sector of a few countries as in the early 1980s.

The volume of capital flight peaked in 1981 and gradually tapered off in the following years. This and an alternative estimate based on preliminary balance-of-payments statistics indicate that capital outflows, which bottomed out in 1986, have been rising for the last two years, although to levels far below those of the early 1980s.

Table 1. Capital flight estimates for highly indebted countries (US$ billions)

	1980-7	1983-7	1986-8
1. Total outflows	−83.7	−30.9	−14.1*
2. Hot money	−77.9	−27.9	−13.5*
3. Residual method	−46.2	−21.6	−8.0
4. Banking assets (deposits)	NA	NA	5.6†
5. Long-term resource inflow	209.8	83.0	33.9
Memorandum item:			
Total outflows / revenues	−39.9%	−37.2%	−42.7%*

Notes: * = 1985-7; † = through September 1988.

Negative sign denotes outflow.

[1] Total outflows: long- and short-term assets of the official, deposit money banks and other sectors plus errors and omissions.

[2] Hot money: short-term capital of other sectors and errors and omissions.

[3] Residual methods: sum of current account, change in reserves, foreign direct investment and net lending.

[4] Banking assets: exchange-rate adjusted changes in BIS reported deposits of the non-bank private sector.

[5] Long-term resource inflow: sum of official transfers, net foreign direct investment and net lending.

Sources: IMF Balance of Payments Statistics, World Bank's Debtor Reporting System, Bank for International Settlements and estimates.

Indeed, only 17 per cent of total outflows occurred during the last three years of the 1980-7 period. Total capital outflows have been heavily concentrated in a few countries, regardless of the measure used (see Table 2).

The private non-bank sector accounted for nearly $42 billion, or roughly half of total capital outflows. Approximately one-third of capital outflows ended up as deposits with commercial banks. Most of the remaining assets, however, were held in a less liquid form and carried rising transaction costs, for example capital market instruments, fixed investments, real estate, art, and so on. This suggests that a large proportion of foreign-held private LDC assets is less susceptible to repatriation in response to short-term incentives in the originating countries, including debt reduction schemes.

The consequences of capital outflows from LDCs were serious. First, the total amount of capital flight was most likely significantly larger than originally estimated. The cumulative value of capital outflows from HICs underestimates their impact on external

Table 2. Capital outflows from HICs (US$ billions)

| | 1983-7 | | | 1986-8 |
	A	B	C	C
Argentina	−1.7	0.6	1.1	2.1
Bolivia	0.6	0.6	1.5	0.3
Brazil	−4.0	−5.5	2.3	−2.2
Chile	0.5	0.2	0.7	0.8
Colombia	−1.8	−2.0	−3.8	−1.5
Cote d'Ivoire	−0.5	0.2	−1.3	−0.1
Costa Rica	0.1	0.5	−0.1	0.2
Jamaica	0.0	−0.3	0.3	0.4
Ecuador	−0.3	0.1	−1.0	−0.4
Mexico	−10.7	−6.8	−17.9	−10.4
Morocco	−0.4	−0.4	0.3	−0.9
Nigeria	−5.1	−7.9	6.8	2.7
Peru	−1.1	−0.9	−0.3	1.6
Philippines	−0.4	−0.7	−2.3	−1.1
Uruguay	−0.1	−0.3	−0.1	−0.1
Venezuela	−6.4	−5.7	−5.5	0.9
Yugoslavia	0.3	0.3	−2.2	−0.4
TOTAL	−30.9	−27.9	−21.6	−8.0

Notes: Negative sign denotes outflow.
  A = Total outflow.
  B = Hot money.
  C = Residual method.

Source: See Table 1.

indebtedness by the amount of capitalized returns retained abroad. Original capital outflows and capitalized earnings (estimated on the basis of the LIBOR interest rate) amounted to $135 billion, between 1980 and 1987. This corresponds roughly to 50 per cent of the total actual change in external debt of HICs during the same period. Secondly, even the originally estimated amount of capital outflows posed a heavy burden on LDC economies. Indeed, developing countries were paying a heavy price for domestic policy distortions. At their peak, at nearly $25 billion in 1981, total capital outflows from all HICs were equivalent to over 2.6 per cent of the aggregate gross national product. However, because a large portion of capital flight was financed with foreign borrowing, capital outflows consumed a relatively modest share of domestic savings.

Firstly the amount of the 1980–7 increase in the stock of foreign assets alone generates an income of roughly $13 billion (calculated at current interest rates), compared to less than $5 billion reported as investment income credits in the HIC current accounts. As foreign creditors stress, foreign financing requirements could be significantly reduced if all the profits from the increase in foreign investments were repatriated.

3. Foreign Lending and Capital Outflows

Our estimates show a very strong correlation between capital outflows and foreign lending. However, we believe that this high correlation does not necessarily reveal conclusive causality linkages in either direction. We argue, however, that the nature of the relationship between net lending and capital flight has changed over time. We also discuss the relationship between net lending and capital flight in the context of risk asymmetries and scarce investment opportunities in developing countries.

Our estimates reveal a close relationship between foreign lending and capital flight. During the 1980–7 period, the total value of capital outflows from HICs ($84 billion) corresponded to roughly 40 per cent of the total net long-term resource inflow to these countries. The link is even stronger with regard to lending (see Figure 1). In the group of high capital-flight countries (Argentina, Brazil, Colombia, Mexico, Nigeria, Peru, Philippines, and Venezuela), for each dollar in net lending, approximately 60 cents was expatriated as capital outflows. This is an important observation given that foreign lending was a major source of foreign exchange reserve financing, and that these reserves were a source of foreign exchange for capital flight.

The correlation between foreign lending and capital outflows can be explained in several ways. For the period prior to 1982, the most straightforward explanation is that governments borrowed to replenish foreign exchange reserves, and, thus, enabled capital outflows. External lending and capital outflows slowed when voluntary lending to developing debtor countries stopped in 1982.

The linkage between capital flight and borrowing changed after the outbreak of payments difficulties in 1982. In particular, the large foreign debt meant that foreign creditors faced much higher levels of risk than before (see Section 7). Foreign lending became scarce and, in the case of commercial creditors, defensive in nature and tied to strong policy conditionality. Disbursements of additional loans were made conditional on the implementation of policies which, by themselves, required less external funding. Therefore, the resulting contraction in lending by 1986, was accompanied by the conspicuous (see Figure 1) reduction in capital flight.

While such a close correlation between lending and capital outflows suggests strong causality, it is just as likely that the decline in capital outflows until 1986 was achieved by better economic policies negotiated in conjunction with lower borrowing requirements and was also due to the imposition of capital controls. The facts corroborate this view; many of the incentives for capital flight, such as the general instability, the debt overhang, and the corroding effects of stagnation already existed by 1986 and yet failed to stimulate outflows. Of course, one cannot exclude the possibility that forms of capital flight changed. For example, export under-invoicing and import over-invoicing, not captured by our capital-flight estimates, could have become a more important source of capital flight.

After 1986, both capital outflows and net lending (propped up by concerted lending arrangements) resumed. However, the role of external lending in funding capital outflows became less obvious and changed from ex-ante financing before the debt crisis to ex-post financing now. Prior to 1982, foreign lending financed foreign exchange reserve accumulation which directly financed capital outflows. Currently, governments allow for capital outflows by falling into arrears. Thus, when they negotiate re-financing of accumulated arrears, foreign lending provides an ex-post financing of capital flight.

Some hypotheses point out that foreign lending caused capital outflows due to risk asymmetries and to scarce investment opportunities. Because foreign lenders, unlike domestic investors, are not subject to expropriation risk, foreign exchange risk, and inflation tax risk, it is efficient to residents of both countries to place claims on a foreign country. It is likely that by offering guarantees, developing country governments helped lower even further the risk faced by foreign lenders and thus indirectly contributed to capital outflows. This hypothesis, though, is more relevant in assessing events in the late 1970s than in the aftermath of the debt crisis.

High Capital Flight Countries
Capital Flight and Net Lending

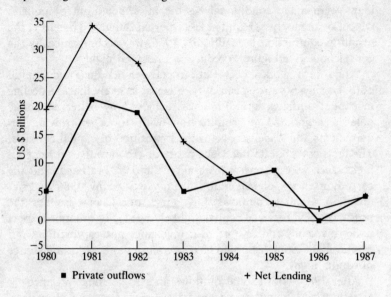

■ Private outflows   + Net Lending

Mexico
Capital Flight and Net Lending

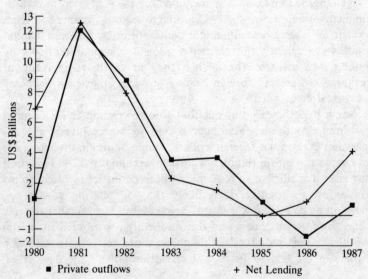

■ Private outflows   + Net Lending

Venezuela
Capital Flight and Net Lending

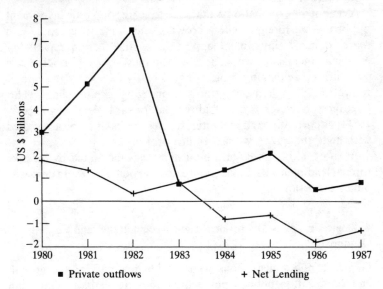

■ Private outflows   + Net Lending

Argentina
Capital Flight and Net Lending

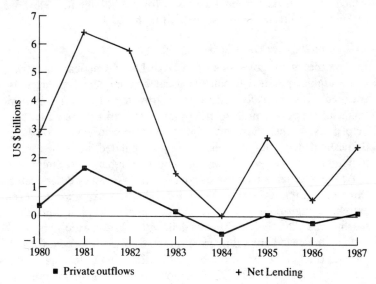

■ Private outflows   + Net Lending

Currently, the risk of default has become at least as important as expropriation risk.

Yet another explanation is that, due to scarce domestic investment opportunities, foreign lending crowded out domestic capital. With scarce domestic investment opportunities and foreign capital financing an increasing proportion of available opportunities, the rate of return on remaining projects could easily fall below the rate of return on foreign assets, thus encouraging capital flight. This hypothesis however, was probably valid for the late 1970s and early 1980s, as currently high real interest rates are likely to be associated with high, though very risky, return projects.

In short, although large capital flight was facilitated by massive foreign lending it was, in fact, more deeply rooted in severe domestic policy distortion.

4. Domestic Policy Distortions, Debt Accumulation and Capital Outflows

Domestic policy distortions were an integral part of the growth and stabilization policies pursued by most large Latin American countries. Policy distortions led to a loss of governments' creditworthiness, exchange-rate overvaluation, and financial instability, which, in turn, generated incentives for capital flight. Below we examine these three factors of capital flight.

Loss of credit-worthiness

During the 1970s, governments of large Latin American countries, for example, pursued expansive fiscal and monetary policies associated with relatively fast rates of growth and received massive financial support from foreign commercial banks. Foreign lending helped avert the short-term inflationary consequences of large domestic deficits, but as foreign debt accumulated, both the foreign and domestic credit-worthiness of these governments were impaired.

As the internal perception of government's solvency deteriorated, thus raising inflationary risks and devaluation expectations, even extremely high interest rates could not prevent capital flight. The reason was that the risk involved in holding domestic debt grew faster than their nominal interest rate and, when corrected for risk factors (including unexpected devaluation risk), foreign assets remained a better choice. Capital flows in and out of the country arbitraged differentials between these risk-adjusted domestic and foreign rates of return.

When risk attached to domestic and sovereign public debt is similar, changes in nominal (risk unadjusted) rates of return on both assets tend to be correlated. Some evidence that real domestic interest rates (corrected for devaluation) and yields on sovereign debt (measured at secondary market prices) have moved in the same direction was found for Chile and, to a lesser extent, Mexico, two debtor countries that made a significant effort to regain their credit-worthiness. An implication of this correlation is that voluntary debt-reduction schemes that lower secondary market discounts could have sizeable beneficial macroeconomic effects on the country by encouraging investment, as the risk factors and real interest rates drop. On the other hand, when government debt repayments fall into arrears, thus raising the secondary market discount, capital outflows are encouraged at least until domestic interest rates adjust to incorporate the higher risk factor. However the correlation between rates of return of domestic and sovereign public debt may have simply stemmed from the link between domestic and foreign interest rates, rather than from the discount in secondary debt markets.

Exchange rate overvaluation

Exchange rate policy was often aimed at fighting inflation rather than at preventing future balance of payments difficulties. For example, in Argentina, Chile, and Uruguay a pre-announced path of decreasing exchange rate devaluations was deliberately enforced to contain inflation. These policies, which were conducted without controls on capital movements, were facilitated by favourable terms of trade, initially low real foreign interest rates and massive foreign lending. These anti-inflation policies led to exchange rate overvaluation and fed capital outflows as speculators bought foreign assets when the real exchange rate became unsustainably overvalued. In this way, central banks financed capital flight, thus rechannelling abroad a substantial portion of foreign lending to governments.

With controls on capital movements, unlike in the open capital account situation described above, currency overvaluation is reflected in a premium the black market offers above the official exchange rate. This tends to raise the unofficial trade surplus, an alternative source of capital flight, because the black maket premium creates an economic incentive for smuggling, export under-invoicing, import over-invoicing, and unofficial transactions related to tourism. Capital flight through smuggling and under-invoicing of exports is also induced by export taxes, or, in the case of drugs, by legal restrictions. On the other hand, import tariffs induce import under-invoicing (as importers seek to avoid trade taxes), that tends to reverse capital flight.

Financial instability

Although financial instability was partly a consequence of fiscal deficits and exchange rate policies, in many countries it was also a by-product of financial repression, that is, of interest rates fixed below inflation rates, high legal reserve requirements of banks, and other institutional rigidities imposed on financial systems. Financial repression encouraged capital flight both by lowering returns on domestic investments and by feeding overall financial instability, for example through its potential impact on financial disintermediation when inflation rises.

In countries with more liberal financial systems, for example with market-determined interest rates, large fiscal deficits and exchange rate overvaluation resulted in high real domestic interest rates, thus creating a different type of financial instability as firms and governments became heavily indebted domestically. Domestic firms that took advantage of relatively cheap foreign credit experienced financial instability after corrective devaluations were implemented. Financial instability also activated what can be regarded as a secondary source of capital flight—the stock of assets held by residents abroad. Financial instability induced foreign asset holders to reinvest abroad the returns on their assets, such as interest, dividends, and capital gains.

While policy distortions tend to have an immediate effect on capital flight, reversing them may only have positive results in the long run. In the short term, trade and fiscal reforms may promote rather than reverse capital flight as they pose a threat to heavily protected sectors, privileged tax loopholes, and tax evasion. However, a substantial reduction of fiscal imbalances could accelerate the beneficial effects of removing other policy distortions.

5. Fiscal Deficits and Capital Flight

The external debt crisis was deeply rooted in domestic fiscal mismanagement. In most countries, fiscal adjustment started after the eruption of the external debt crisis and centred around reductions in public investment and (to a lesser extent) in real wages and consumption. However, it did not suffice to close the widening fiscal gap and, thus, gave way to an internal transfer problem. The internal transfer refers to the transfer of resources from the domestic private sector to the public sector to finance government expenditures. The internal transfer problem has become a cause of capital flight because of the looming tax liability that poses a threat to resident's domestic wealth. Here we examine how governments' efforts to circumvent the internal transfer problem have actually aggravated capital flight.

When conventional tax (or non-tax) revenue cannot be raised and foreign credit is no longer available, governments try to finance their deficits by printing money or issuing bonds at a high cost. When they issue bonds, the growth of domestic debt quickly becomes unsustainable, as high interest rates lead to an explosive growth of the domestic debt service. Thus, this form of finance soon reaches a ceiling. Domestic debt accumulation beyond that ceiling raises explosively the risk of inflationary taxation and, along with it, of a large devaluation, since further increases in domestic debt have to be monetized. Similarly, due to its impact on inflation, printing money to finance the deficit also has a ceiling. The ceiling is given by the inflation level beyond which massive capital flight and monetary and financial disintermediation take place. In short, governments' ability to increase domestic financing of fiscal deficits is seriously undermined by the adverse macroeconomic consequences which high capital mobility may bring about.

To alleviate mounting fiscal pressures, various forms of external debt relief and debt rescheduling have been used by developing country governments. For example, in Brazil and Mexico external debt rescheduling of publicly guaranteed private debt has often coincided with continuing repayment by the private sector of those debts to the central bank. In this way, governments generate finance, as they appropriate private repayments of foreign debt in exchange for the responsibility for servicing private external debts but at a later date. Of course, in the long run, this 'socialization' of private foreign debt aggravates the internal transfer problem. The positive impact of this type of government finance is also conducive to capital flight because, by substituting foreign financing for domestic financing of deficits, it leads to exchange rate overvaluation.

Alternatively, countries use arrears on foreign debt to alleviate the internal transfer problem. However, exercising the arrears option encourages capital flight due to its adverse impact on country risk, as reflected in a growing secondary market discount on sovereign debt.

Yet another way of financing the internal transfer could be through external debt reduction schemes. Foreign debt reduction, by lowering the public foreign debt service, can help close the fiscal gap. However, under some circumstances this option would not yield the expected results. For example, countries that have already exercised the arrears option, and which, therefore, do not make any payments to creditors, cannot make any cash-flow gain from debt reduction. Neither will they improve their external credit-worthiness unless, of course, debt reduction is large enough to reverse the unwillingness of debtors to service-their debts.

Some schemes of voluntary foreign debt reduction may even have an immediate adverse effect on the internal transfer. For example, swaps of private equity for public debt, which amount to an anticipated repurchase of foreign public debt, have to be financed by issuing money or domestic debt.

In short, domestic policy distortions prevalent in the late 1970s and early 1980s were the most important incentive for capital flight in most highly indebted developing countries. However, while domestic policy distortions appear to be the dominant cause for capital outflows, there are some other factors of capital flight which are less dependent on domestic economic policies.

6. Other Factors of Demand for Foreign Assets

From a microeconomic point of view, demand for foreign assets can be explained in terms of optimal portfolio allocation analysis. According to this approach, agents choose assets which maximize the expected rate of return on their portfolio, given their risk preferences. In particular, this analysis requires consideration of international portfolio diversification strategies and opportunities arising from growing LDC involvement in international economic activities. Institutional factors such as foreign exchange controls or capital movement restrictions may raise the risk and / or the cost of demanding foreign assets, but once those risks and costs are quantified they become parameters of the optimal investment decision.

Risk diversification involves a variety of interrelated dimensions: political risks such as expropriation; external risks, like terms of trade changes; and economic distortions such as inflation. The boundaries between risk dimensions may be quite tenuous. For example, high inflation, which usually reflects the lack of political will or the power to lower fiscal deficits, often becomes a mechanism for domestic capital expropriation and / or for taxing the poor (political risk dimension). All risks are magnified by domestic policy distortions, thus strengthening incentives for capital to flee. In pursuit of desirable policy goals, governments often attempt to eliminate one distortion by allowing other distortions (and the associated risks) to worsen. For example, measures taken to combat inflation through exchange rate appreciation amplify the impact of other risk factors, such as a deterioration in the terms of trade.

Developing countries became over time increasingly engaged in international economic activities that require investing and holding working balances abroad. This growing openness to the world economy caused a similarly irreversible approach to international portfolio diversification.

Capital flight is also a response to the more promising development of investment opportunities abroad. They were all the more striking when compared to underdeveloped domestic capital markets. Competition in international capital markets reduced transaction costs and raised the quantity and quality of financial assets available. By contrast, in many indebted developing countries, regulated interest rates, high legal reserve requirements, and stock markets heavily oriented towards government bond issues have raised transaction costs and limited investment opportunities in the private sector. Finally, during the 1980s the economic performance of OECD countries and the newly industrialized Asian countries, boosted by fast productivity increases and superior investment opportunities, was better than in most highly indebted countries. This explains why foreign markets provided higher and more stable returns which enticed capital flight.

Aside from the traditional domestic and external factors encouraging capital flight, new factors have emerged following the onset of the debt crisis.

7. Debt Overhang, Uncertainty, and Capital Outflows

The large foreign debt accumulated by developing countries has also become a factor of capital flight. One explanation of why a large debt encourages capital flight is based on the investment disincentive effect of the debt overhang. However, we favour an alternative hypothesis which stresses the role of uncertainty stemming from the large foreign debt.

It is argued that the mere size of the external debt creates disincentives for investment, or economic policy adjustment, because the fruits of the additional effort are entirely appropriated by foreign creditors. Debt service payments would act as a very high marginal tax on investment. This is the 'debt overhang' hypothesis, which states that debt discourages domestic investment, thus creating an incentive for capital flight.

The most evident counter-example to the 'debt overhang' hypothesis is Chile, which has one of the largest debt-to-GNP ratios, a record of hefty debt service payments, a strong investment and growth record, and low levels of capital outflows. One reason the 'debt overhang' hypothesis may not account for the Chilean experience is the failure of this hypothesis to incorporate the uncertainty costs of default.

Therefore, we offer an alternative explanation for capital flight, based on the uncertainty created by a high level of foreign debt. Uncertainty stems from the impact of future debt service on the orientation of domestic economic policies. A large debt can lead to domestic-policy instability due to the unpredictability of the outcome of frequent debtor / creditor negotiations and the impact of the fiscal burden associated with the foreign debt on the internal political struggle for scarce fiscal resources. A large foreign debt service-makes economic policies more unstable because, with a shrinking fiscal pie, political struggles tend to intensify.

The fact that most of the foreign debt constitutes a liability of the public sector strengthens incentives for capital flight under the 'uncertainty' hypothesis. The private sector in most HICs is healthy financially but does not assume responsibility for the public sector debt. The major relevant difference between private and public sector debt is that private sector debts can be settled with some kind of market discipline, either through repayment or liquidation of borrowing firms. Public sector debts, on the other hand, have to be serviced with taxes. But because there is a great deal of uncertainty with regard to future fiscal policy the instability that public foreign debt creates is translated into stronger incentives for capital flight.

A large foreign debt can also raise uncertainty due to the short-lived nature of debt restructuring arrangements, which projects an aura of instability. Frequent changes in these arrangements adversely affect expectations with regard to fiscal and monetary policies and make them subject to extended bargaining. In the process, many debtors get away with partial default, while creditors, who are engaged in defensive lending to protect their existing investments, eventually approve (ex-post) the *status quo*. This, of course, perpetuates incentives for capital outflows.[1]

8. Conclusions and Policy Recommendations

The central conclusion of this paper is that capital flight has not only been a cause but, more importantly, a consequence of the domestic fiscal crisis plaguing highly indebted developing countries.

Facilitated by massive foreign lending, in the early 1980s capital flight was encouraged by large fiscal deficits and fixed exchange rate policies. Although fiscal imbalances were underlying the 1982 external debt crisis, and to a large degree were made possible by abundant foreign lending, they became evident only after the crisis erupted.

The reduction of government deficits (excluding debt service), and real exchange rate devaluations, along with the drying-up of foreign credit, explain why capital outflows were declining through 1986. However, as fiscal imbalances were still large, domestic sources of deficit finance gradually gained importance. As a consequence, the deterioration of governments' external credit-worthiness soon translated into a loss of domestic credit-worthiness.

The deterioration of governments' credit-worthiness led to a resumption of capital flight after 1986, despite the introduction of foreign-exchange controls. The impact on capital flight of the loss of credit-worthiness was compounded by greater domestic policy instability associated with the large accumulated foreign debt. Policy instability stemmed both from the uncertain outcome of frequent debtor–creditor negotiations, and from a deepening of political struggles originated in the competition for scarce fiscal resources. As a consequence, risk premia attached to returns on domestic investment increased. Capital flight became a mechanism for arbitraging out differentials between risk-adjusted domestic and foreign rates of return.

The following policy recommendations for creditors, policy-makers, and residents stem from our analysis:

1. Foreign creditors should press for the removal of domestic policy distortions. The elimination of these distortions should prove beneficial to creditors and debtors alike. Debt relief schemes should be limited to debtor countries that are willing to regain both domestic and external credit-worthiness. Lack of debtors' commitment to restore credit-worthiness is likely to be associated with low levels of investment, capital flight, and an intractable fiscal situation.

2. For domestic policy makers, the main message is that private capital mobility has severely limited their ability to conduct domestic macroeconomic policies. In particular, capital flight has penalized those governments which neglected the removal of domestic policy distortions and, especially, those which ignored the importance of preserving their domestic and external credit-worthiness.

3. For residents, including those who hold foreign assets, pressing for structural reforms should become a matter of self interest. Until those reforms are implemented, one way of minimizing the long-term costs for the country of accumulated private foreign assets could be for residents to employ those assets to engage in the creation of multinational firms. The creation of such firms could, at least, help the country preserve or even improve its entrepreneurial talents while allowing it to develop existing or potential comparative advantages.

To conclude, developing countries could not escape the world trend towards greater international capital mobility. Capital outflows from developing countries are a proof of the failure to adapt to this trend.

Notes

[1] Both the 'uncertainty' and the 'debt-overhang' hypotheses seem to support the Argentine experience, with its dismal investment record.

Export Risk and Capital Movements: The Theory of Asset Swapping

SPECIAL MERIT AWARD

Editors' Introduction

Traditional theory states that the instability of LDCs' export earnings has restricted their savings and investment and therefore slowed development. World Bank economist John Nash sets out to show the limitations of this approach. Using the framework of modern portfolio theory, the author argues that, as long as it is possible for domestic savers to diversify this risk and for foreigners to take on some of the risk, resource utilization will be maximized. One of the main barriers to risk diversification in developing countries is the existence of capital controls, which stop both purchase of foreign assets by domestic residents and inward investment by foreigners. The essay concludes that empirical studies which establish a link between export instability and low levels of savings and investment have only done this in cases where there was no way to diversify the risk, that is, where there were restrictive capital controls. The author thus seeks to stress the very high economic costs of restricting long-term capital flows.

John D. Nash, Jr., 36, is currently a research economist with the Trade Policy Division of the World Bank. His areas of research interest include issues relating to reform of trade policies in developing countries, the effects of instability in prices and earnings of primary export commodities, and mechanisms to mitigate the adverse effects of this instability. Issues related to export instability was the topic of his doctoral dissertation at the University of Chicago, completed in 1982. His professional positions have included assistant professor at Texas A & M University (from which he received a BA), assistant director and economic advisor to the Chairman of the Federal Trade Commission, and economist with the Agricultural Operations Division for Mexico and Central America of the World Bank. In 1984 he received the Federal Trade Commission Award for Economic Excellence. He has published in several leading journals as well as contributing chapters to two books on the connection of the macro economic and agricultural sectors.

7

Export Risk and Capital Movements: The Theory of Asset Swapping

JOHN D. NASH Jr

1. Introduction

Few governments in the developing world allow capital to flow freely across the borders of their countries. Many impose severe restrictions, if not outright prohibitions, on foreign investment in their economies, as well as investment abroad by domestic savers. The former restrictions are usually justified as an attempt to prevent neo-colonialist exploitation or protect 'strategic sectors'. The latter are frequently imposed for macroeconomic reasons—to control capital flight or the money supply or to resolve balance of payments difficulties. While there has been for some time ample evidence that they do not work well for these purposes (Haberler, 1975) they continue to be used.

One point that is often lost in the macroeconomic framework in which the debate over capital controls has been conducted, is that capital transactions of all kinds have microeconomic foundations. Modern portfolio theory (and evidence) have clearly demonstrated that one major motivation for purchases of particular assets is to diversify risk. Risk is a source of great concern in developing countries. In particular, it has often been asserted that the high risk from fluctuations in primary export prices and earnings has adverse effects on these countries' savings and investment behaviour. Yet, surprisingly, the connection has not been made between this risk and the consequent capital flows.

This essay argues that the excessive risk from export instability only has detrimental effects when either domestic savers cannot invest in foreign assets or foreign savers cannot invest domestically. Otherwise, if the capital account is open, there may be asymmetries in portfolios, but no distortions in the economy will be introduced by the risk. For policy makers, this argues that capital account controls are more costly than is commonly realized.

2. Background: The Debate on Export Instability

Through the period of the early 1960s, most economists who held any opinion on the matter had an unquestioning faith in the proposition that instability of the export prices (and earnings) of less-developed economies was one of the reasons why they failed to develop. From Cairncross's *Factors in Economic Development* (1962): 'The prices of primary products are notoriously volatile, and the damaging effects of this volatility on the economies of the exporting countries are beyond question.'

In the absence of any definitive empirical work, the chain of reasoning used to support the above conclusion began with the observation that the exports of most LDCs are concentrated in a relatively small number of agricultural or mineral products, resulting in larger fluctuations in aggregate export prices and earnings than would be the case if they were more diversified. For a variety of reasons (well catalogued by MacBean, 1966), both the demand for and supply of these commodities were presumed to be quite price inelastic compared to those of manufactured goods. Furthermore, the supply of agricultural crops was thought to be extremely volatile because of the vagaries of tropical agriculture, which used few modern inputs designed to minimize the effects of climatic fluctuations and other natural disturbances. And the demand for industrial inputs (like metals, rubber, and jute) was believed to fluctuate in response to business cycles of industrialized countries. It was generally assumed, implicitly or explicitly, that stocks of the primary commodities were small or non-existent. The combination of volatile and inelastic supply and demand, small stockpiles, and a lack of diversification on the part of each LDC meant that each country faced export prices (and earnings) that were inherently unstable.[1]

The next link in the logical chain was the assertion that this extreme variability is somehow detrimental. The arguments to this effect revolved around an assumption of risk aversion on the part of some economic agent, and the conclusion that worthwhile investments would be passed up because of the uncertainty stemming from export instability. Batra (1975), for example, argued that if export prices are more unstable than domestic, then resources will tend to gravitate to the less risky sector. So, the equilibrium expected marginal product of factors in the export sector will exceed that in the domestic sector, meaning that national product is not maximized. A second variation on the theme is that export earnings instability creates uncertainty in the supply of foreign exchange, needed for domestic and export sector capital imports (Hawkins, Espstein, and Gonzales, 1966). This disrupts planning of the government (McNicol, 1978) or private entrepreneurs (MacBean, 1966) and deters investment in this way.

This, then, was the state of the theoretical discussion regarding export instability before 1960. The conclusion was that it was bad, everyone knew it was bad, and attention should be turned to ways to eliminate it. Historically, a number of schemes were proposed to try to stabilize the prices of commodity exports; perhaps one of the best known was the 'commodity reserve currency' supported by Jan Tinbergen, among others. Beginning in the early 1950s, the United Nations became actively involved in the attempt to develop solutions to this problem. These efforts later evolved into a call for the establishment of an Integrated Programme for Commodities by the UN Secretariat in 1974, one element of which is a group of buffer stocks for certain primary commodities (Mayall, Laursen). While the IPC has finally been agreed upon, it has yet to begin to function. The advisability and feasibility of stabilizing prices has been the subject of much debate, even apart from the effects on fluctuations in earnings.[2] Other programs that have actually been put into operation to offset variability of exchange flows are the STABEX scheme run by the European Community to benefit former European colonies and the Compensatory Finance Facility of the IMF.

Notwithstanding the attention and effort devoted to devising ways of mitigating the pernicious effects of export instability, the empirical work done since 1960 has been far from unanimous in condemning it as a culprit in suppressing development. A veritable potpourri of results has been generated in the attempt empirically to link instability to development (Coppock, 1962; Glezakos, 1973, 1984; Kenen and Voivodas, 1972; Knudsen and Parnes, 1975; Knudsen and Yotopoulos, 1976; MacBean, 1966; Maizels, 1968; Savvides, 1984; and Voivodas, 1974). Some studies have found the expected negative correlation, some have found no relation, and some have even found a positive correlation. This discrepancy between theory and empirical findings has been a major paradox.

3. Asset Swapping

An understanding of how domestic and international capital markets interact to share risks, combined with elements of modern portfolio theory, can shed much light on this puzzling departure of reality from theory. It can also provide a better understanding of the reason for the commonly observed phenomenon that foreign investors have historically tended to own a disproportionately large share of export-oriented primary production. Far from being evidence of neo-colonialist exploitation, as some have alleged, this seems to be simply a rational response to a certain asymmetry in capital markets.

Suppose, as is commonly believed, that the risk of investing in the traditional export sector is significantly higher than that of investing in the domestic sector. But the relevant risk from the viewpoint of the investor is that which cannot be diversified away by an appropriate portfolio composition. The non-diversifiable risk of an asset is determined by the degree of covariance between its return and those of others that can be put in the portfolio. If the export sector is really riskier, it must be because returns in this sector are highly correlated with those of other available assets. The risk, therefore, depends fundamentally on what assets are available for diversification. This, in turn, depends on the nature of capital controls.

If the capital account is closed, and the only assets available are domestic, say, risk-free treasury bonds and stocks in the domestic market, there will be an equilibrium risk premium over the risk-free rate necessary for returns on investment in the export sector. The size of this risk premium will vary directly with the covariance between returns in the export sector and those on a basket of domestic stocks.[3] This covariance is likely to be large, since there are strong connections between the two sectors, implying that their cycles will be closely linked. For one thing, the availability and cost of imported inputs for domestic industry depends to a large extent on export earnings. Also, export income affects the demand for domestic products. Swings in foreign exchange earnings (and therefore in the monetary base) may generate domestic business cycles. The large risk premium reduces overall levels of savings and investment, since even when partially compensated by shifting the portfolio toward risk-free assets or domestic stocks, the risk lowers the welfare of savers. The risk especially depresses investment in the export sector. Economically worthwhile projects will be passed over in this sector, and, in turn, the sector will be 'too small' relative to the domestic sector, consistent with the argument in previous literature. The greater the export instability in this case, the greater the inefficiency of investment allocation, and the smaller the export sector relative to the domestic.

This result, however, is inconsistent with an open capital account. If foreign savers have access to the domestic asset market, while domestic savers can buy foreign assets, arbitrage will take place between the two markets. Foreign savers investing in export assets may be exempt from certain risks to which domestic savers would be susceptible, such as exchange risk. Foreign markets offer much greater opportunities for domestic savers to diversify risks that are non-diversifiable when the only alternatives are domestic stocks or export-sector assets. While there are links between certain export sectors (such as ores) and business cycles in world markets, the diversity of assets available on world markets should ensure that risk even in these sectors can be substantially reduced by appropriate portfolio selection. The premium of the required return in the export sector relative to the risk-free rate will thus be lower with the open capital account. Furthermore, the 'wedge' between the return on the domestic- and export-sector assets can be shown to be proportional to the difference between the covariance of the former with a basket of international assets and that of the latter with this basket. Since both of these covariances are likely to be low, and the difference between them small, the outcome of opening the capital account is that the difference between the returns in the two sectors (the cause of the inefficiency in inter-sectoral investment allocation) is removed, and with it the systematic artificial reduction in size of the export sector.

The mechanism by which the arbitrage is effected is essentially a swap of assets between foreign and domestic savers. Foreign savers buy export-sector assets, in a sense displacing domestic savers from this market. Domestic savers, having the option of diversifying their portfolios by purchasing assets that have low covariance with domestic sector and export sector assets, will do

so, and will be better off because of it. Consequently, the degree
of export instability will not affect the total quantity of asset
holdings by domestic savers. Neither will it affect the total volume
of investment. Projects that are 'worthwhile', that is, that have a
positive net present value at the market discount rate (not including
a risk premium), will be done. Since it does not depress either
domestic savings or investment, export instability should have no
effect on national welfare or growth. This resolves the apparent
puzzle of the inconsistency between earlier theories and the failure
to find the expected negative relation between instability and
savings, investment, or growth. The negative relation holds only
for economies with closed capital accounts, and previous studies
have not attempted to draw the distinction in their empirical tests.

On the other hand, there is some reason to suppose that the
instability may affect the composition of portfolios. If, for example,
some risks associated with a foreign sector are more readily
diversified by foreign investors, or risks associated with the domestic
sector are more easily diversified by domestic savers, each would
'specialize' by holding a disproportionate share of assets in the
sector where he can most easily diversify risks. This would then
explain the phenomenon alluded to earlier, that historically foreign
investors have tended to own disproportionate shares of the
relatively risky primary-export sectors.

One can think of a number of reasons for such an asymmetry
in the ease with which risks can be diversified. First, domestic
savers may not have costless access to foreign-asset markets. If
markets for information about foreign assets are not well developed,
as is likely in developing countries, it may be difficult to find out
the covariance of returns among different types of assets. Transaction costs in dealing with brokers may be high. For example,
savings must be converted to foreign exchange to purchase foreign
assets and then back into local currency when the savings are
liquidated for consumption, with the usual costs of converting
between currencies. Many savers in developing countries may be
tied to local markets by custom, making it costly to deal in
foreign-asset markets. As a result, part of the risk that is readily
diversifiable for foreign savers is diversifiable for domestic savers
only at some costs. For this reason, the relevant risk of investment
in the export sector as perceived by domestic savers is greater than
that perceived by foreign savers, and the equilibrium portfolio

share of these assets is correspondingly smaller. The greater the undiversifiable risk (or transaction cost) becomes, the more domestic savers reduce their holdings of export assets, and the greater is the share of investment in this sector done by foreign savers. Foreign savers in general would be expected to be more familiar with markets for internationally traded goods than with markets for goods produced for domestic consumption. For them, transaction costs in dealing with assets of the domestic sector may be higher than for domestic savers. In this case like that outlined above, foreign savers will in equilibrium hold a disproportionate share of export assets, and domestic savers a disproportionate share of domestic assets. But it should be emphasized that even in these two cases of market asymmetry, arbitrage still keeps the risk premium for the export sector low or zero, ensuring that resources are allocated efficiently, that is, in such a way that rates of return between the sectors are (approximately) equal. These asymmetries simply produce a corresponding asymmetry in the ownership of assets.

Of course, there is no reason why 'asset-swapping' should occur only in response to the particular kind of risk created by export instability. Its implications are clearly much broader, applying to situations where the riskiness of investment comes from other sources, as well. This whole concept has a considerable a priori appeal because of the casual empirical observations that many of the obviously high-risk, export-oriented projects in developing countries (for example in agriculture and mineral production) are undertaken by foreign investors, and that in situations of high risk, domestic savers tend to invest in foreign assets (Schultz, 1976). But export instability is an easily measurable kind of risk, and provides a good opportunity to test the hypothesis.

4. Asset Swapping: The Evidence[4]

While it is easy to find specific examples of asset swapping occurring, it is much harder to test in a more general way. The difficulty arises because asset swapping only works to the extent that capital is free to flow between domestic and international markets. In a particular country in a particular year, the capital account may be completely free, completely restricted (that is, with domestic savers not allowed to purchase foreign assets and foreign savers not allowed to invest

domestically), or something in between, and this status has in some
countries been changed quickly and with great frequency. The key
to looking at the issue empirically in a cross-section context is to
find a reasonably lengthy time period when a sample of small
economies simultaneously maintained open capital accounts. The
last such period ended around 1960,[5] as determined by a search
through the IMF's publication *Exchange Restrictions*, published
yearly since 1950, which contains information—country by country—on all types of capital account restrictions, including those on
long-term and direct investment. Thus, the data are unfortunately
somewhat dated, but since they cast some light on a hypothesis
with contemporary policy implications, they should be of more
than purely historical interest.

Two aspects of the theory of asset swapping are discussed here—
the mechanism and the end result. The mechanism was empirically
examined using a sample of countries with unrestricted capital
accounts from 1950 until sometime after 1960.[6] The end result was
examined by comparing the structures of these economies to the
structures of a sample of countries with restricted capital accounts.
Since the sample of 'unrestricted' countries is small and there is no
presumption of linearity in the relations being examined, two
nonparametric statistics (the Spearman rank-order coefficient and
the modified Olmstead–Tukey statistic recommended by Conover,
1979) were used in addition to the more usual regression analysis.

The mechanism through which 'asset swapping' works has
implications for the relationships between export instability and
three economic variables. Specifically, instability should have no
negative effect on saving nor total investment, but should be
positively correlated with the fraction of investment which is foreign
in origin. Using the two measures of instability and three statistical
measures of correlation, there is no evidence of a significant negative
correlation between instability and the propensity to save.

The effect of instability on the investment rate (the ratio of
investment to GDP) was also tested. Since some investigators have
predicted that instability should depress investment through its
effect on the private sector, while others have claimed that the
impact should be on government investment, total gross domestic
fixed-capital formation was used as the investment variable. The
results indicated that, as expected, instability has no negative
impact.

Finally, the hypothesis that instability is positively related to foreign investment, as a fraction of total investment in the economy, was tested. All of the measures of correlation with the standard instability index were positive, and the two non-parametric statistics each showed a high degree of significance. In the test for positive correlation with the Knudsen–Yotopolos index, two of the three statistics were of the 'correct' sign, though the significance levels were not as convincing as in the test using the standard instability measure. The reason for the partial discrepancy in these two sets of results may be attributable to the difference in the two instability indices. The Knudsen–Yotopolos index is a measure of short-term instability, while the standard instability index is a better measure of long-term instability. For a variety of reasons, short-term instability creates less risk than long-term, and furthermore, the kind of risk which it does create would be more easily compensated by domestic investors.[7] Since the whole motivating force behind 'asset swapping' is the displacement of domestic by foreign investment to compensate for the risk created by instability, it would be expected that the swapping would not occur in response to instability which does not create so much risk, that is, short-term instability. And this is, in fact, what was indicated here.

Next, consider the implication of 'asset swapping' for theories regarding the investment rates and consequent sizes of the domestic and export sectors of the economy. Some have asserted that if instability and risk are greater in the export sector, this will cause the equilibrium size of this sector to be 'too small', and that of the domestic sector to be 'too big'. These hypotheses do not, of course, assert that risk is the only, or even the primary, determinant of the relative sizes of the sector: only that there is a systematic relationship (see Batra, 1975 for an example of this type of analysis). However, in those countries where assets can be 'swapped' between domestic and foreign residents (that is, countries with no restrictions on long-term capital flows, including direct investment), the equilibrium sizes of the sectors need bear no relationship to their relative riskiness. This difference between countries with and without restrictions on capital flows can form the basis for a test of asset swapping. If the hypothesis is true, in countries with no restrictions on capital flows, the relative sizes of the export and domestic sectors should be uncorrelated with their relative indexes of instability, while in countries with such restrictions, the correlation should be negative. The results of such a test—comparing ratios of domestic-to export sector instability and domestic to export sector size for countries with restricted and unrestricted capital accounts, using each of the two measures of instability and using three statistical measures—showed clear evidence of a strong negative correlation for the restricted sample, and no such evidence for the non-restricted. The net result of an open capital account seems to be as the asset-swapping theory would predict.

5 Conclusions and Policy Implications

The main conclusion of the theory of asset swapping is that neither savings nor investment need be stifled by risk, if domestic residents are able to 'swap assets' with foreign investors. Of course, this requires an open capital account, since foreign investors must be allowed to take on high-risk projects which would otherwise deter domestic investment, and domestic savers must be able to accumulate foreign assets with the assets they would otherwise invest domestically. This simple observation may help to explain why the empirical studies of the effect of instability on development have been inconsistent in their findings. The mechanism by which instability generates inefficiency in resource-use only operates to the extent capital-account controls prevent asset swapping, and this is not taken into account in the empirical studies.

But more importantly to policy-makers, it underlines the economic cost of restricting long-term capital flows. Restrictions on foreign investment in the domestic market mean that some high-risk projects—particularly in the export sector—are not undertaken, if the risk premium required by the domestic capital market is too high to make the projects feasible. Restrictions on accumulation of foreign assets by domestic residents may face them with the option of putting their savings in high-risk national projects, or not saving as much. The first type of restriction thus depresses overall marginal investment and diverts it away from the export sector, while the second reduces marginal savings. Either type is harmful in the long run, not only because it discourages capital accumulation, but also because it encourages the resource misallocation that comes from differences in risk among sectors. This was illustrated by comparing the relation between instability and relative sector size in countries with capital-account restrictions and those without.

An open capital account, of course, is not a panacea for all problems that may result from export instability. It would not alleviate the fiscal difficulties that may be caused by fluctuations in government revenue from export taxes.[8] Long-term capital flows would not offset the short-term destabilization of the domestic sector that may occur as fluctuations in foreign-exchange earnings are reflected in changes in the monetary base (short-term capital flows, however, can do this quite effectively—see Nash, 1982). Finally, an open capital account will not allow small producers with no access to capital markets to diversify their risks. In this sense, it is not a substitute for a well-functioning futures market or other risk-reducing mechanisms.

It will, however, create the opportunity for savers to diversify risks, and so will reduce the risk premium (and the equilibrium interest rate) required on loans to small producers. This will directly benefit the producers while enhancing efficient inter-sectoral resource allocation.

Given the pervasive nature of such restrictions in less-developed countries, especially of the type that prohibit domestic residents from accumulating foreign assets (see Swidrowski, 1975, or the IMF's annual *Exchange Restrictions*), it is very important to weigh all of the costs. Some of the costs have been ably explained by other investigators (Mills, 1975; Haberler, 1975). However, the costs and benefits of open capital accounts have too often been debated as a solely macroeconomic issue. As in other economic fields, where the distinction between micro- and macroeconomics has become increasingly blurred, so it is here. The implications of modern portfolio theory is that some capital flows, particularly long-term, have microeconomic foundations. The failure to recognize this has meant that the debate has been carried out without acknowledging that closing the capital account interferes with asset swapping, which is an economy's natural mechanism for minimizing the adverse effects of export instability or other factors that cause economic risk. For less-developed countries that feel that risk induced by export instability (or other factors) is a problem, this is a cost that should be seriously weighed.

Notes

[1] For a survey of literature on the causes of export instability, see Knudsen and Parnes (1975).

[2] A recent survey of issues and state-of-the-art analysis of the implications of price stabilization is contained in Newbery and Stiglitz (1981).

[3] Nash (forthcoming) contains a technical exposition of this argument.

[4] Nash (forthcoming) describes the statistical tests and results in more detail.

[5] Unfortunately, in this period, international capital markets were not as well developed as they now are, and access to some industrial countries' capital markets (particularly in Europe) was restricted to some degree. If anything this biases the empirical results against a positive finding of asset swapping. Or, alternatively, it means that the mechanism would work more efficiently in today's environment of more efficient markets.

[6] The sample of thirty-eight countries used by Knudsen and Yotopoulos (1976) was divided into 'restricted capital account' and 'non-restricted capital account' sub-samples by the criterion described in the text. This criterion placed the following countries in the 'unrestricted' category: Bolivia, Costa Rica, Dominican Republic, Ecuador, El Salvador, Guatemala, Mexico, Panama, Paraguay, Peru, and Uruguay.

[7] For example, short-term export instability is more easily 'filtered out' by short-term capital flows before it destabilizes the domestic sector and the exchange rate. Economic agents can more easily borrow to offset short-term down-turns in earnings than long term. Also, short-term instability in export prices causes smaller variance in the value of a total benefit stream of a project that depends on that export than does long-term instability (Nash, 1982).

[8] Other mechanisms may be useful for this purpose, such as the revenue-stabilization fund (used in Chile for copper) or buffer funds (used in Papua New Guinea for agricultural exports).

References

Batra, Reveenra N. (1975), *The Pure Theory of International Trade Under Uncertainty* (London: The Macmillan Press Ltd.).

Conover, W. J. (1979), *Practical Nonparametric Statistics* (NY: John Wiley and Sons, Inc.), pp. 336–40.

Coppock, J. D. (1962), *International Economic Instability* (NY: McGraw-Hill).

Erb, G. F., and S. Schiavo-Campo (1969), 'Export Instability, Level of Development and Economic Size of Less Developed Countries', *Bulletin of Oxford University Institute of Economics and Statistics* (November), 31: pp. 263–678.

Glezakos, C. (1973), 'Export Instability and Economic Growth: A Statistical Verification', *Economic Development and Cultural Change* (July), 21: pp. 630–78.

—— (1984), 'Export Instability and Economic Growth: Reply', *Economic Development and Cultural Change* (April), 32: pp. 615–23.

Haberler, G. (1975), 'The Case Against Capital Controls for Balance of Payments Reasons', in A. K. Swoboda (ed.), *Capital Movements and Their Control* (Geneva: Institut Universitaire de Hautes Études Internationales).

Hawkins, R., J. Epstein, and J. Gonzales (1966), 'Stabilization of Export Receipts and Economic Development—International Commodity Agreements and Compensatory Financing Plans', *The Bulletin* of New York University (November) no. 40.

Kenen, P. B., and C. S. Voivodas (1972), 'Export Instability and Economic Growth', *Kyklos*, fasc. 4, pp. 791–804.

Knudsen, O., and A. Parnes (1975), *Trade Instability and Economic Development* (Lexington: Lexington Books).

Knudsen O., and P. Yotopoulos (1976), 'A Transitory Income Approach to Export Instability', *Stanford Food Research Studies*.

Laursen K. (1978) 'The integrated programme for commodities', World Development Vol. 6, pp. 423–35.

MacBean, A. L. (1966), *Export Instability and Economic Development* (Cambridge, Massachusetts: Harvard University Press).

McNicol, D. L. (1978), *Commodity Agreement and Price Stabilization* (Lexington: Lexington Books).

Maizels, A. (1968), 'Review of Export Instability and Economic Development', *American Economic Review* (June), 58: p. 575.

Massell, B. F. (1964), 'Export Concentration and Export Earnings', *American Economic Review* (March), 54: pp. 47–63.

—— (1970), 'Export Instability and Economic Structure', *American Economic Review* (September), 60: pp. 618–30.

Mayall, J. (1980) 'The pressures for a new international commodity regime' in G. Goodwin and J. Mayall (eds): *A new international commodity regime* (St Martin's Press, New York).

Mills, R. H., Jr. (1975), 'An Evaluation of Measures to Influence Volatile Capital Flows', in A. K. Swoboda (ed.) *Capital Movements and Their Control* (Geneva: Institut Universitaire de Hautes Études Internationales).

Nash, J. D. (1982), 'Long-Term and Short-Term Export Instability, and an Extra Cost of Restrictions on Capital Movements', (unpublished manuscript).

—— (forthcoming), 'Export Instability and Long-Term Capital Flows: Response to Asset Risk in a Small Economy', *Economic Inquiry*.

Newbery, D. M. G. and J. E. Stiglitz. (1981), *The Theory of Commodity Price Stabilization: a Study in the Economics of Risk* (Oxford: Clarendon Press).

Olmstead, C. S., and J. W. Tukey (1947). 'A Corner Test for Association', *The Annals of Mathematical Statistics*, 18: pp. 495–513.

Savvides, Andreas (1984), 'Export Instability and Economic Growth: Some New Evidence', *Economic Development and Cultural Change* (April) 32: pp. 607–14.

Schultz, T. W. (1976), *Transforming Traditional Agriculture* (New Haven: Yale University Press), pp. 87–8.

Swidrowski, J. (1975), *Exchange and Trade Controls* (Epping, Essex: Gower Press Ltd.); see especially pp. 135–6, 193–6.

Voivodas, C. S. (1974), 'The Effect of Foreign Exchange Instability on Growth', *Review of Economics and Statistics* (August) pp. 410–12.

Aid for Business in Developing Countries: Who's Doing What and What More Should be Done?

SPECIAL MERIT AWARD

Editors' Introduction

Assistance for developing countries, both loans and grant aid, has been too heavily concentrated on the public sector and project lending, argues Cory Highland of the OECD. This is changing because most of the top performing LDCs have relied on the private sector to catalyse growth and development. While relatively little of the large amounts of external assistance goes to benefit the private sector directly, the author highlights the recent change in the World Bank and OECD towards policy lending and enterprise development. He argues that OECD donors are still too concerned about aid volume, but that they are examining more closely the question of aid effectiveness through private sector development programmes. Mr Highland urges donors of aid to lend more to support adjustment and reform rather than for public projects, and to pay greater attention to the needs of the private sector.

The author recognizes that reliable infrastructure and public services are important for a healthy economy, but argues that aid donors and the World Bank could make more effective use of their resources by helping to create favourable business conditions in developing countries.

Cory Highland, 32, is an economist at the OECD Secretariat in Paris, where he has just written a book, *International Cooperation for Private Enterprise and Investment in Developing Countries*, to be published in January 1990. A *magna cum laude* graduate of Temple University, Mr Highland holds a Master's degree from Columbia University and is on the faculty of the American University of Paris, where he teaches international economics. He was awarded a study tour of Japan in 1989 for his winning entry in the OECD Japan Essay Contest.

8

Aid for Business in Developing Countries: Who's Doing What and What More Should be Done?

A. CORY HIGHLAND*

1. Introduction

Since the early 1960s the international community has grappled with poverty, malnourishment, and illiteracy in developing countries. While progress has been made, underdevelopment remains one of the most intractable problems in the international economy. The term 'developing countries' is itself confusing, because some of these countries are not developing but stagnating. A few are even regressing. Countries that have managed to move forward contrast sharply with those left behind.

What makes development happen? Traditional development doctrine holds that natural resources, geography, climate, and market size—all factors a country cannot control—largely determine a country's development. Poor countries progress only when the rich help them overcome these handicaps. Development happens when resources are transferred from the 'haves' to the 'have nots'. The goal of development policy is to increase aid to give governments the wherewithal to feed, clothe, educate, and house their people. This thinking dominated the development agenda for over two decades.

A new strategy has emerged in the last few years which challenges this orthodoxy. It is based on numerous country experiences in which businesses competing in open markets have catalysed broad-based economic development. The new strategy emphasizes better resource use, not just greater resource volume. The objective is not only to mobilize more resources, but to use those resources more effectively. A great many developing countries, including

* The views expressed in this paper are those of the author and they do not represent the position of the OECD, World Bank Group, or of any other group.

those in the low-income bracket and those who have relied on government-led growth, are trying to give business a larger role in development. Aid donors and multilateral lenders also extol the benefits of the private sector.

This paper is about how external agencies try to promote enterprise and investment in developing countries. It argues that donors and multilateral agencies are trying to give greater support to private businesses but that they still rely too much on government projects and the public sector. Suggestions are made on how to improve private sector programmes. The paper focuses on OECD bilateral donors and the World Bank Group: the OECD because they provided over 80 per cent of world aid in 1987, and the World Bank because it is in the best position to embrace the private sector (see OECD, DAC Report 1987–8: p. 11).

2. Business-Led Growth: Old Problems, New Opportunities

A country's human, capital, and natural resource base, private-sector history, and development level will all affect the rate at which private enterprise and investment can promote development. That Venezuela's per capita income is about twice the Latin American average is obviously related to its rich oil deposits. Countries like Brazil and Mexico can probably be more optimistic about their futures than Haiti or El Salvador, in part because their national markets are rich enough to support a varied industrial and agricultural base. In the very poorest countries, some of the fundamental requirements for a strong private sector are missing: basic education and training, entrepreneurial drive, management, legal and accounting skills, and even basic infrastructure. International agencies play a particularly important role here. Beyond natural endowments, political, social, and cultural factors are also important. Costa Rica's superior performance in Central America is clearly linked to its strong tradition of stable government and a culture that places a high premium on education and enterprise.

As important as these factors are, good policies and institutions are even more critical to development. A country's growth potential is determined largely by how effectively the authorities create a business-compatible economy. As the Asian newly industrialized countries and others have shown, even small countries with few natural resources and fragmented markets can use business and investment to launch economic development.

Sound economic and regulatory policies are the starting points not only for business and investment but for economic growth generally. Good private-sector policies constitute good development policies. Macroeconomic policies, particularly pricing policies, are critical to business. A regulatory system that protects private assets, treats investors equally, allows free movement of resources, and guards against monopolies has no substitute. Countries that have followed this strategy and helped businesses develop have fared better than those that have not. This is as true for Subsaharan Africa—where countries showing the best performance tend to have active private sectors (Kenya, Malawi, Mauritius)—as it is for East Asia, where businesses have helped the region grow more than twice as fast as any other in recent years.

New opportunities for market-led growth are opening in many developing countries. Local entrepreneurs have grown in number and influence, creating a private sector constituency which did not exist before and enabling them to play a greater role in the economy. Private industrial and financial institutions have become more sophisticated, making it possible to undertake some of the large projects that were traditionally considered beyond their scope. And domestic capital markets are beginning to come of age in a few developing countries, mobilizing savings and increasing opportunities for privatization. The capital markets in Brazil, Malaysia, India, Korea, and Taiwan have grown between $10 and $70 billion each, and are today comparable to European markets.

LDCs recognize that business is important to development, but they face formidable obstacles in trying to change to a market-oriented system. Over-regulation is typically an inherent feature of developing economies, and rules governing trade, finance, competition, and labour frustrate entrepreneurial growth. High tariffs and quantitative restrictions promote and maintain monopolies, and overvalued exchange rates make it difficult for local businessmen to export. Credit to business is limited by exchange-allocation systems which give government enterprises first claim on scarce financial resources. In fourteen of the thirty-five African countries studied by the IMF, for example, the public sector's share of outstanding domestic credit exceeds 60 per cent (Marsden, 1987, p. 26). Financial market regulations undermine small enterprise lending and discourage equity savings and fledgling stock exchanges and investment banks. Private participation in activities such as mining, manufacturing, and public utilities is proscribed in many LDCs. And payroll taxes, high social security charges, exorbitant lay-off penalties, and rigid collective bargaining rules frustrate new worker hirings and the use of part-time workers. Wage and bonus schemes are rarely linked to productivity or profitability, but are rigidly set through sector-wide bargaining or national law.

Those who can change the system often have the least interest in doing so. Ministers and civil servants who control state-owned enterprises do not want to lose the privileges that authority brings. Labour unions are afraid that more competition will lead to lay-offs. The military may oppose efforts to loosen state control over strategic industries. Urban dwellers will resist the higher food prices that follow agricultural liberalization. And the private business élite may not wish to surrender their protected position in the economy. Taken together these groups can be a potent political force.

3. The OECD Donors and Private Sector Development

Who gives aid and what are they doing for business and investment in developing countries?

The OECD is home to the most important donor group in the world, the Development Assistance Committee, or DAC. As the oldest and only group comprised exclusively of aid donors, DAC's role in private sector development is crucial. Its eighteen Members account for 80 per cent of world aid. In 1987 alone they gave or lent developing countries and multilateral institutions almost $42 billion, which was over half the total net financial flows to developing countries that year. If less concessional but still below-market monies are counted, the figure rises to 70 per cent. DAC aid levels have been growing, too, by about 3.5 per cent over the past decade, and they are expected to continue to grow. Last year, for example, DAC's aid grew almost 7 per cent in real terms to over $47 billion (OECD Press Release, 1989, p. 1). Compared to multilateral institutions, too, the DAC's contributions are enormous: its members gave developing countries three times as much assistance as the multilaterals last year, a ratio which has remained constant throughout the 1980s.

DAC members' impact on developing countries is powerful. Few of the poorest countries derive less than 10 per cent of their GNP from external sources, and many get more than 25 per cent. Foreign assistance can comprise as much as 60 per cent of a country's budget. In relative and absolute terms DAC's role in the Third World is substantial. It is the pre-eminent player in the aid business. Institutionally DAC is an important body. It is one of the OECD's oldest committees and the only one to have a full-time chairman. It is also the only committee to have its own think-tank, the OECD Development Centre, which publishes research on development problems.

DAC members are uniquely positioned to facilitate Third World business development, not only because of the money they can provide, but because of their long experience in developing countries. Many donors have developed reliable partnerships with leading decision-makers and bureaucrats, and they are trusted and in a good position to assist in business-led development. Field missions understand a bureaucracy's strengths and weaknesses and can provide practical, 'on the ground' advice on how to overcome administrative bottle-necks. Untapped and under-used skills, re- sources, and manpower can be targeted, mobilized, and revitalized.

Much of what donors already do—build houses, schools, and hospitals and train teachers, farmers, and doctors—indirectly helps the private sector. Businessmen need roads, rails, and ports to obtain inputs and to market their products, and a healthy and literate work-force is an asset to any business. Information flows depend on reliable communications, and production is impossible without dependable energy supplies. Donors help build the in- frastructure and human resources that businesses need.

In the past, and to some extent today, donors tended to cluster around government projects. Aid was, and still remains, a government business. Food, money, and technical assistance pass from one government agency (or government-sponsored agency) to another. In fact, only official transactions can be counted as aid. Development purists have argued that aid should not go directly to private business because it would give the beneficiary an unfair advantage. Besides, how would businesses to receive aid be chosen? These difficulties did not seem to apply, however, to state enterprises, many of which stayed in business with aid money and enjoyed tremendous advantages over competitors.

Another problem bilateral donors encounter in business-led

development is that relatively few aid professionals have the practical training, experience, or expertise to help build a business. And donor-business contact has been sporadic. It was only recently that business development was regarded by some donors as a legitimate form of assistance. This is not unique to the OECD group. Other external agencies are trying to inject fresh thinking into the development debate through new approaches which highlight the private sector. The World Bank's reorganization will give greater focus to policy reform and business development. The Inter-American Development Bank has just formed a private-sector arm, the Inter-American Investment Corporation, to increase lending to the private sector. And the Asian Development Bank is reorienting its activities towards private business.

The OECD is shifting its focus too, even though much of its development work continues to centre on official resource transfers. A large number of DAC meetings still revolve around aid volume, and most of the secretariat's time is spent measuring how much and from whom aid is flowing. Two working parties have been set up for this purpose: one on statistics, which measures and monitors aid volume, and another on financial aspects of aid, which measures aid 'purity'.

Nevertheless, the OECD is moving beyond these traditional activities to give greater emphasis to the private sector. Donors have instituted a number of programmes to support business-led development. Many of these programmes have been discussed at the OECD and a new study on aid's role in business will be published by OECD this year. Donors are helping move credit to the private sector through local development banks, by opening up central-bank credit lines for on-lending by local intermediaries, and by supporting institutions that lend to small businesses. Germany, the Netherlands, and Sweden have launched partnerships between their commercial banks and lenders in developing countries. Japan and others provide cheap loans for joint enterprises. Donors have also established promotional agencies, management-development centres, and business-advisory services to help raise productivity and management and marketing skills. Germany subsidizes firms to train LDC managers, Sweden subsidizes technology transfer, and the US gives grants for management and technical training, and has helped in privatization and foreign-investment promotion. To promote exports, aid agencies give firms training grants, funding for feasibility studies, and loans. They also assist trade-promotion centres and other institutions responsible for export development. Donors encourage investment to developing countries through investment guarantee and joint venture schemes, bilateral investment and double taxation treaties, and information and promotion services. Several OECD countries have programmes under which developing country products can enter their markets duty-free.

All of these activities are designed to help stimulate business and investment in developing countries. There is increasing recognition among individual OECD donors, and in the DAC collectively, that business's role in development deserves greater emphasis.

4. The World Bank and Business

The World Bank has been helping governments with policies to facilitate competition and efficiency for ten years. Through its policy dialogue and adjustment lending, the Bank helps recipients minimize the costs of financial, legal, and institutional reforms which are needed to attract foreign investment and stimulate local entrepreneurs. Structural and sectoral adjustment programmes have helped restore market disciplines in a number of countries. Loans in Burundi, Senegal, Pakistan, and Dominica, for example, are designed to abolish, streamline, or liberalize investment regulations and procedures. Jamaica reduced red tape and stabilized its foreign-exchange allocations system with World Bank help. In Turkey, Bank loans facilitated duty-free imports, made domestic credit more available, and enabled a review of mining, petroleum, and tourism laws to promote foreign private investment.

The Bank has not always placed such great emphasis on improving business opportunities in developing countries: only 13 per cent of total lending went to policy reform from 1981–7 (Shirley, 1988, p. 42). Infrastructure loans totalled almost half of the Bank's lending during the same period, which is how the Bank indirectly helped business. Its traditional approach was to transfer resources through loans for roads, dams, bridges, and so on. Loan volume was the main standard by which success at the Bank was measured; after all, the Bank's core business is lending, not economic policy. Increasingly, though, the Bank is linking its lending to policy improvements. Indeed, the Bank must provide resources to make its leadership credible. Money must accompany policy advice if the dialogue between the Bank and borrowers is to continue. And loans enable the Bank's staff to learn about the borrowing country's economy.

What is happening today is that the Bank is using more of its resources and influence to improve private business prospects through policy reform. The Bank's private sector activities are moving beyond support for rural development and credit to enterprises through financial intermediaries, which together accounted for 25 per cent of Bank lending between 1981 and 1987. One of the reasons is that lending to business through financial intermediaries, many of which are government owned or controlled, has proved difficult. Many local development banks suffer from government interference, weak management, over-dependence on donors, and inability to mobilize funds. More than a few are bankrupt or near-bankrupt, and they survive only with regular infusions of donor capital. The situation is so grim in Africa that the Bank considered setting up its own financial intermediaries there, but decided against it.

The Bank is also shifting its adjustment lending to accommodate the private sector. Structural adjustment loans now focus more explicitly on private sector policies, and sector loans are reducing restrictive regulations on agriculture and industry. The Bank is using sector loans to restructure inefficient programmes and policies, and is paying closer attention to institutional reforms in adjustment lending, an area where the Bank has been weak. It is also working harder to ensure that borrowing countries adhere to adjustment programmes. More use is being made of 'tranching', whereby the borrower must take specific actions before monies are released. In other cases, borrowing countries are taking action even before requesting a loan.

Even the Bank's traditional activities in industry, infrastructure, and public services are becoming more private sector oriented. Lending to public industrial enterprises was cut back from 7 per cent of total lending in 1981 to 0.7 per cent in 1987, and recent projects are likely to emphasize restructuring, not new investment. Contracting out, management contracts, and privatization are becoming more common in the Bank's infrastructure projects. And the Bank has been studying how to privatize public services like housing and urban busing.

The Bank's private-sector activities are also covered by the

International Finance Corporation (IFC), and the Multilateral Investment Guarantee Agency (MIGA).

The IFC advises on policies and regulations to facilitate foreign investment in developing countries, provides technical assistance to local entrepreneurs, and helps governments develop their financial markets. But, like the Bank's private-sector programmes, these activities have traditionally represented a small portion of IFC's portfolio. Of the IFC's 300 professionals only a handful work primarily on policy issues. The rest lend or arrange loans for private sector projects. IFC makes equity investments too, but its loans exceed investments by a 4-to-1 margin, and that multiple is increasing. The IFC is tiny compared to the World Bank: its 300 professionals hardly compare to the Bank's 3,000. IFC investment since its creation totals $10 billion. The Bank disbursed almost $15 billion last year *alone* (World Bank Annual Report, 1988, p. 9).

Again, this situation is changing as the IFC gives greater emphasis to policy advice-and support in its private-sector work. It is focusing more on corporate restructuring and privatization, and has set up a new unit for this purpose. It has also expanded its technical and advisory services in Africa and the Caribbean to help local businessmen attract outside capital. In another IFC scheme 'company doctors' from businesses like IBM, Nestlé, and Barclays help revitalize ailing African corporations. IFC continues to expand its efforts to develop local capital markets by advising and investing in them. Since 1971 the corporation has undertaken more than 350 investment and advisory projects in over seventy countries (Sethness, 1988, p. 32). This assistance has included advice on tax laws, financial regulations, and investor protection policies. The effort has been successful: by the end of 1987, the largest stock markets in nineteen developing countries had grown to an aggregate total market capitalization of about $180 billion. Some of these emerging markets are comparable in size to the smaller European markets, and many have been growing much faster than European markets over the past decade.

MIGA, an independent agency of the World Bank, will help developing countries attract foreign investment by insuring against non-commercial risks, and by advising governments on programmes and policies to facilitate foreign investment. MIGA was inaugurated only last June, so it is too early to tell how successful it will be. Initially MIGA will concentrate on the insurance end of the business and leave the advisory function until later. It has already received applications to cover some $1 billion worth of projects in mining and manufacturing (*Financial Times*, 2 March 1989). The Bank has said that it would be at least a year before it could focus on MIGA's consultancy function, but MIGA and IFC have already merged the investment advisory service into a single unit.

The World Bank Group is changing. The reorganization is giving greater focus to private enterprise and the conditions needed for business to grow. With its command of concessional finance, its mandate to deal with long-term development, its country-specific and international capacity for research, and ten years of experience in policy reform, the Bank is better suited for the job than any other international institution.

5. What Else Can Be Done?

How can the World Bank and OECD donors further promote business and investment in the Third World?

They can broaden support for business-compatible policies and avoid those that undermine enterprises. Programmes that restrict competition might be curtailed and eliminated, and the resources reprogrammed for policy reform. New aid and loans should be conditioned on the institutional, regulatory, and policy reforms that businesses need to survive and grow. This constitutes the most important element of private-enterprise development. Programmes for investment and export promotion, and assistance to local enterprises will fail if the policies and institutions are wrong. Donors and the Bank should spend more on policy reform and less on projects that cannot be sustained in a bad policy environment. Policy adjustments in countries like Chile, Costa Rica, Ghana and Thailand have enabled firms there to grow and export. Devaluation has made exporting more profitable, trade liberalization has made it easier to import parts and export goods, and deregulation has created a freer business climate. The relative success of privatization in countries like Chile, the Ivory Coast, and Malaysia is due mainly to improvements in the business climate.

In addition to general policy reform, donors and the Bank should continue to do more to rationalize parastatals and privatize public services. Progress in either of these areas will open up substantial business opportunities.

Many state enterprises are suffering chronic losses from bad management, overstaffing, and political interference. They frequently account for over 10 per cent of a country's gross domestic product. By 1980, almost half of the ninety countries tracked by the IMF were pumping more than one-third of their GDP into the public sector. Now that their budgets are drained, LDCs are hoping the private sector will take over in areas traditionally reserved for the state. In the last five years over eighty governments have announced support for privatization, but progress has been slow. For every five privatizations announced only about one takes place. The same economic and political problems that drove state enterprises under prevent them from being privatized. Thus, in Brazil only a few unimportant state-owned enterprises have been privatized, in Zaire the enterprises involved were mostly small farms, and in Mexico less than 1 per cent of its parastatal assets have been sold.

Privatization can be expensive. Costs typically involve redundancy and severance payments, advisory services, and restructuring and rehabilitation costs. Donors should play a bigger role in offsetting these costs. Aid agencies should spend more on advisory services needed in analysing enterprises selected for reform. Redundancy payments could be underwritten with external support, and workers retrained and relocated. Donors and lenders could scale down and terminate subsidies for loss-making enterprises, then help identify potential buyers. Private management could be appointed with outside help. Inefficient public services could be scaled down further, and their functions transferred to private operators. Much of this is already happening but more could be done. In Brazil and Argentina for example, donors helped privatize road construction and maintenance, and in Kenya private drivers compete freely with the state bus company.

In all of their enterprise development efforts, agencies should systematically consult business about which particular policies and institutions need reform. Donor-business contacts need to be broadened. External agencies can strengthen their capacity for meaningful reform only if the private sector is involved in policy discussions. Businessmen know their strengths and weaknesses best, and donors must tap this pool of expertise. In this way surprises are avoided, stability is enhanced, and business and government can operate with a reasonable degree of certainty. Business participation in policy discussion should also lead to stronger consensus on development objectives, a better understanding of policy options, and less resistance to reform which the recipient country's private sector might feel are against its interests—tariff and quota reductions, for example.

The OECD as an institution is trying to play a greater role in private-sector development. It should continue to move beyond the focus on aid volume and spend more time examining aid effectiveness. The amount of resources committed to a project does not determine success. The strategies pursued, the effectiveness of organization, and the allocation of resources are determinative. Levels of input are important, but it is the way in which they are committed that is crucial. Here is where the private sector is important.

When donors review each others' programmes, more attention should be given to the private sector. Too little time is spent during aid reviews on the private sector, even for those countries in which the private sector plays an important part. For example, donors should discuss their experiences in specific aspects of private-sector development such as policy and parastatal reform, and privatization of public services. Donors who have assisted in policy reform should explain which particular reforms—trade, tax, labour, and so on—they were able to facilitate by their assistance. What kinds of assistance—grants, technical assistance, finance, and so on— proved particularly effective in inducing reform, and why? Was business brought into the dialogue and if so, at what stage? The same questions should be discussed by those who have engaged in reforming parastatals and public services. What was the best reform tool—technical and financial assistance, placement / retraining support, and so on? Which alternatives to total divestiture seem most promising—partial divestiture and / or closures, management contracts, leasing arrangements? Which public services offer the best possibilities for private participation?

These questions should be discussed by donors. A group whose members give 80 per cent of world aid and provide over half of the developing world's financial inflows is vital to the private sector.

The World Bank recognizes that it needs to do more in private-sector development. It is lending more to change policies, regulations, and laws that retard private business and investment.

The Bank is also taking a more direct role in privatization, and its economic and sector work is giving greater attention to private provision of public services. IFC is expanding its capital market work, even as the Bank is lending more for financial sector reform. The Bank is also trying to develop new approaches to private-sector development through better research. Lending will continue as the Bank's major activity, but loans and assistance are increasingly geared toward policy reform and the private sector.

6. Conclusion

The primary goal of a nation's development strategy should be to improve the conditions of life, income, and employment for its people. Economic goals such as growth, higher productivity, and lower inflation are a means of achieving these objectives, not ends in themselves. It has become obvious that profit-based businesses competing in open markets have catalyzed broad-based development across a wide spectrum of countries. External agencies are trying to do more for business and investment in the Third World. Development depends on it.

References

Asian Development Bank (1989), *The Asian Development Bank in the 1990s: Panel Report* (January).
—— (1988), *Asian Development Review: Studies of Asian and Pacific Economic Issues*, 6, no. 2.
Cassen, Robert, and others (1986), *Does Aid Work?: Report to an Intergovenmental Task Force* (Oxford: Clarendon Press).
Far Eastern Economic Review, 'Debt Crisis and Reaganomics Give IFC a New Lease of Life', 29 September 1988, pp. 107–8.
The Economist, 'Africa: Blooming Entrepreneurs', 1 April 1989, p. 72.
Financial Times, 15 September 1987; 20 February 1989; 2 March 1989.
Harrison, Lawrence E. (1985), *Underdevelopment Is a State of Mind: The Latin American Case* (Lanham, Md.: The Center for International Affairs, Harvard University, and University Press of America).
Krueger, Anne O. (1988) (ed.) *Development with Trade: LDCs and the International Economy*, Sequoia Seminar Publication (San Francisco: ICS Press).
—— (1989), 'The Role of Multilateral Lending Institutions in the Development Process', *Asian Development Review*.

Lewis, W. Arthur (1961), *The Theory of Economic Growth* (London: George Allen & Unwin Ltd.)

Magaziner, Ira C., and Robert B. Reich (1983), *Minding America's Business: The Decline and Rise of the American Economy* (New York: Random House, Inc., Vintage Books).

Marsden, Keith (1987), 'Private Enterprise in Africa', *World Bank Discussion Papers* (July) p. 26.

Morawetz, David (1977), *Twenty-Five Years of Economic Development: 1950 to 1975* (Washington, DC: The World Bank).

Organization for Economic Co-operation and Development (OECD) (1988), *Aid Co-ordination and Aid Effectiveness: A Review of Country and Regional Experience*, by A. J. Barry, Development Centre Papers (Paris: OECD).

—— (1987–8), *Development Co-operation: Efforts and Policies of the Members of the Development Assistance Committee, 1987–8 Report* (Paris: OECD).

—— 'Financial Resources for Developing Countries: 1988 and Recent Trends', press release (Paris, 16 June 1989).

—— (1987–8), *Financing and External Debt of Developing Countries*, 1986–7 Surveys (Paris: OECD).

—— (1987a), *Interdependence and Co-operation in Tomorrow's World*, a Symposium Marking the Twenty-Fifth Anniversary of the OECD (Paris: OECD).

—— (1987b), *International Investment and Multinational Enterprises: Recent Trends in International Direct Investment* (Paris: OECD).

—— (1985), *Twenty Five Years of Development Co-operation: A Review*, by Rutherford M. Poats, Efforts and Policies of the Members of the Development Assistance Committee 1985 Report (Paris: OECD).

Overseas Development Council (1988), *Strengthening the Poor. What Have We Learned?* by John P. Lewis and contributors, US–Third World Policy Perspectives, no. 10 (New Brunswick, NJ: Transaction Books).

Pearson, Lester B. (1969), *Partners in Development: Report of the Commission on International Development* (New York: Praeger Publishers).

Pfeffermann, Guy, and Dale R. Weigel (1988), 'The Private Sector and the Policy Environment', *Finance and Development*, 25, no. 4 (December), pp. 25–7.

Roberts, Paul Craig (1989), 'A Tale of Two Countries: Why Chile Booms As Peru Swoons', *Business Week*, 29 May, p. 9.

Roth, Gabriel (1987), *The Private Provision of Public Services*, EDI Series in Economic Development (New York: Oxford University Press).

Ryrie, Sir William (1988), 'An Investment Bank for Development', excerpts from a speech made at the Annual IFC Luncheon in West Berlin, 16 September, 1988; *The Bank's World* (November), p. 18.

Sethness, Charles O. (1988), 'Capital Market Development', *Finance and Development* (December), p. 32.

Shirley, Mary (1988), 'Promoting the Private Sector', *Finance and Development*, 25, no. 1 (March), pp. 40-3.

Singer, H. W. (1987), 'Food Aid: Development Tool or Obstacle to Development?' *Development Policy Reviews*, 5 pp. 323-39.

Trade Finance (1989), 'Deals & Projects: Turkish Power: BOT Firing on All Cylinders' (April), 4.

The World Bank (1988), *Adjustment Lending: An Evaluation of Ten Years of Experience*, Policy & Research Series (Washington, DC: The World Bank).

—— (1988a), Annual Report 1988 (Washington, DC: The World Bank).

—— (1986), 'Developing-Country Stock Markets After the Crash: Growth and Volatility', *World Bank News* VII, no. 44 (17 November), pp. 3-4.

—— (1989), 'The Private Sector Challenge', *World Bank News*, VIII, no. 18 (4 May) pp. 5-6.

Structural Reform and Debt in Africa

SPECIAL MERIT AWARD

Editors' Introduction

Jeffrey Herbst of Princeton argues that, while African countries are beginning to reform their economies, the changes in policies are not enough, as continuing high levels of external debt 'compromise their economic prospects'. Recognizing this constraint, many proposals have been made to reduce these countries' debt burden. The author argues that the need to tie debt relief to good economic policies is often overlooked. Much of the progress so far, in economic reform, has been in response to the incentive of continuing flows of finance. Debt reduction could have the unintended effect of removing this incentive. In underlining this part of his thesis the author describes the 'logic' of poor economic policies in many African countries in terms of the political needs of the rulers. Many African governments, lacking tax revenues, have maintained support through direct intervention in markets, for example foreign exchange markets, state companies, and agricultural pricing. The author recommends that while debt reduction is necessary it should be phased in gradually, contingent on continuing economic reform and meeting strict performance criteria.

Jeffrey I. Herbst, 28, holds a Ph.D Degree in Political Science from Yale University (1987). He is currently Assistant Professor at Woodrow Wilson School, Princeton University, where he is giving courses in economic policymaking in Africa, and on relations between industrialized and developing countries. He completed a Woodrow Wilson School project on privatization in Africa. As a Fulbright Research Associate in 1986-7, he conducted research on economic policy at the University of Zimbabwe, Harare, for eighteen months. In 1989 he was a McNamara Fellow (of the World Bank) undertaking research in Ghana on economic adjustment.

9

Structural Reform and Debt in Africa

JEFFREY I. HERBST

Throughout the African continent*, governments are beginning to attempt to reform their economies in order to decrease public sector inefficiency, reduce price distortions, and restore the viability of the agricultural sector. African countries have been driven to make these reforms in good part because they cannot receive any more funds even from official creditors unless their programmes for economic reform are approved by the International Monetary Fund (IMF). However, even with these programmes of economic reform, it is doubtful if most African countries will be able to grow quickly enough to avoid debt levels that will compromise their economic prospects for the foreseeable future.

Therefore, many proposals have recently been made to lessen the debt burden of African countries by forgiving loans, postponing due dates, or providing new flows of capital. Unfortunately, while these proposals are well-intentioned and address an important problem, by not tying debt relief to continued economic reform the suggestions may have the unintended effect of decreasing the need many leaders in Africa feel to reform their economies. This is especially true because poor economic policies, while disastrous for African economies, provide important political advantages to African leaders. After reviewing the political logic of poor economic policies in Africa, I will make a series of proposals that will tie economic reform directly to debt reduction. Such a link is desirable because it will mean that African governments will continue to have incentives to reform but will now have the knowledge that if they do adjust their economies, economic change will mean more to their citizens than just having more money with which to pay their creditors.

* This paper will focus on Africa south of the Sahara, excluding South Africa.

Jeffrey Herbst

The Political Logic of Poor Economic Policies in Africa

African economies have performed extremely poorly over the last fifteen years. Between 1970 and 1979, Gross National Product per capita increased across the continent by only 0.8 per cent a year and fifteen countries had negative per capita growth rates (World Bank, 1981: pp. 2–3). Between 1980 and 1988 per capita income across the continent actually *decreased* by 0.8 per cent each year assuming, as the World Bank does, that the overall population growth rate is 3.2 per cent (World Bank, 1986: p. 57 and UNDP and World Bank, 1989: p. 6). There are many reasons for this poor performance and there has been a wide-ranging debate as to the exact amount of blame that should be assigned to domestic factors or the depressed international economic environment that Africa has confronted for the last fifteen years. However, there is now a widespread consensus that the poor economic policies adopted by African countries have contributed a great deal to the current crisis and that these policies must change before African countries can grow again.

It is important to understand why poor economic policies were adopted in the first place throughout Africa. The crucial point is that these policies were adopted not because of poor advice or simple errors but because they make political sense given the political systems that almost all African countries have. Most African leaders operate in political systems where votes do not matter. Instead, rulers try to institutionalize their regimes by establishing webs of patron–client relations to garner the support necessary to remain in power. However, African governments are often not able to make direct transfers to those they would like to reward because of their weak tax bases. Indeed, given their dependence on import and export taxes, African countries as a group probably have the weakest tax bases in the world (Anderson, 1987: p. 6). As a result, it is sometimes extremely difficult for leaders to reward important constituencies with direct transfers or the kind of 'pork barrel' projects that are so familiar in the West. Instead, African regimes often rig markets through direct state intervention in order for resources to flow to constituencies important to their continued tenure in office. To illustrate the political logic of state intervention in African markets, I will examine three areas that the World Bank (1981: p. 4) noted were in need of significant reform in its major 1981 document *Accelerated Development in Sub-Saharan Africa*: the public sector, exchange rates, and agricultural policies.

The paradigmatic example of state intervention in the economy to cement patron–client relations is the state-owned enterprises which blossomed throughout Africa as soon as countries began to receive their independence in the 1960s. For instance, in Tanzania, public enterprises went from eighty in 1967 to 400 in 1981 (d'Almeida, 1986: p. 56). Similarly, public enterprises in nominally capitalist Kenya increased from twenty at independence to sixty in 1979 while parastatals went from virtually zero in Ghana to over 100 in the early 1960s. Other countries such as Zambia, Tanzania, Senegal, Mali, Côte d'Ivoire, Mauritania, and Madagascar also experienced tremendous growth in their public-enterprise sectors (Hyden, 1983: p. 97; Nellis, 1986: p. 56; F. Constantin *et al.*, 1979; Dutheil de la Rochère, 1976: pp. 49–51). Accordingly, Short's data suggest that the share of public enterprises in the Gross Domestic Product of African countries is roughly twice as high as in developing countries generally (17.5 per cent compared to 8.6 per cent) and that African public enterprises share in gross fixed capital formation is roughly 20 per cent higher (32.4 per cent versus 27.0 per cent) than in the average developing country (Short, 1984: p. 118).

Indeed, state-owned corporations are a particularly good source of patronage for African leaders because they can employ (by African standards) large numbers of people, direct important resources to specific areas, and operate in greater secrecy than the government in general. As early as 1962, the Coker Commission found that the Action Group in Western Nigeria was siphoning off money from parastatals to fund political activities (Coker Commission, 1962). Since then, control of public enterprises has become an important part of the power structure for many African leaders. As Dennis A. Rondinelli, John R. Nellis and G. Shabbir Cheema note (1984: pp. 1–2),

Many political leaders emphasize the primacy of the public sector, which provides positions in the civil service-and parastatal institutions with which to reward loyal political followers. They keep under central government control those factors—such as wages, prices, tariffs, food subsidies, and import and export regulations—that are considered to be most important for maintaining political stability. Clearly, policies promoting centralization usually pay off, at least in the short run, in material and political returns for the dominant elites.

However, precisely because they are such good conduits for patronage, African state-owned enterprises have been exceptionally poor performers since independence. Not surprisingly, their political functions cause African state-owned enterprises to be 'pressured to increase employment, to deliver outputs at low prices to key groups, and to shape investment decisions other than with economic and financial returns in view' (World Bank, 1981: p. 38). What little systematic analysis there is suggests that African state-owned enterprises have performed extremely poorly. For instance, in one study of West African countries, 62 per cent of the public enterprises showed net losses while 36 per cent had negative net worth (Nellis, 1986: p. 17). Similarly, a study of state-owned transport enterprises in eighteen francophone countries found that only 20 per cent generated enough revenue to cover operating costs, depreciation, and finance charges; 20 per cent covered operating costs plus depreciation; 40 per cent barely covered operating costs; and a final 20 per cent were far from covering operating costs. Thus, in Kenya the average rate of return of public enterprises was 0.2 per cent while in Niger the net losses of public enterprises amounted to 4 per cent of the country's GDP in 1982 and in Tanzania in the late 1970s one-third of all public enterprises ran losses (Nellis, 1986: p. 20). Other studies indicate that in Benin, Mali, Sudan, Nigeria, Mauritania, Zaïre, Sierra Leone, and Senegal public enterprises have accumulated losses which sometimes amount to a significant percentage of the total economy (Nellis, 1986: pp. 17-19).

The second area where African governments have tended to intervene in the economy for political reasons has been the import regime. Countries have two basic ways of controlling imports so that they do not exhaust their foreign exchange reserves: the market (that is a correctly valued exchange rate) or administrative controls (for example tariffs and quotas). African countries have consistently chosen to control imports administratively in large part because this type of import regime offers them far more political benefits. Under a market-determined import regime, no importer can be discriminated against, because all face the same prices. However, in a system of tariffs and quotas, a government is able selectively to allocate import licenses, and apply different levels of protection to different industries in order to reward clients. Indeed, in impoverished African countries, allocation of an import permit is almost a licence to print money because those few who are able to bring in foreign goods will be assured of making a large profit.

Unfortunately, reliance on an administrative system to control imports almost inevitably leads in practice to an overvalued exchange rate. If leaders rely on administrative controls rather than the exchange rate to ration imports, they do not feel compelled to adjust the exchange rate to reflect differences between domestic inflation and the inflation rates of their trading partners. Indeed, in a perverse manner, use of administrative import regimes actually encourages ever-increasing overvaluation of exchange rates because the more the exchange rate becomes overvalued, the greater the benefit a government can bestow on those few who gain access to foreign goods. As the World Bank noted, 'Governments have relied increasingly on import restrictions rather than devaluation to conserve foreign exchange. More and more countries have imposed higher tariffs, quotas, and bans on "nonessential" imports. Quantitative restrictions have been the favoured means of import restriction' (World Bank, 1986: p. 24).

As is now well recognized, these overvalued exchange rates have a significant deleterious impact on African economies. The overvalued exchange rates make it extremely difficult for exporters to remain competitive in world markets that are priced in US dollars. The World Bank noted in 1981 that 'trade and exchange rate policy is at the heart of the failure to provide adequate incentives for agricultural production and for exports in much of Africa' (World Bank, 1986: p. 24). Overvalued exchange rates are particularly damaging for African countries because exports account for such a high percentage of the total economy. Exports of goods and non-factor services accounted for 23 per cent of Gross Domestic Product across all of Sub-Saharan Africa in 1979 compared to 20 per cent for all middle-income countries and 11 per cent for all low-income countries (World Bank, 1986: p. 147).

The third area where African governments have widely intervened for political reasons has been agricultural producer prices. African governments have consistently adopted monopsonistic systems to buy food from peasant growers. The price is set by the government, often below the true market price, in order to subsidize urban consumers who are politically important to African regimes.

Peasants are usually unable to pressure the government to change prices because they are fragmented, the state has the ability to crush most rural protests, and the state's control of the marketing system as well as the supply of inputs allows it to give selective 'side-payments' to potential leaders of rural protests in order to buy them off (Bates, 1981). As is now well known, these low producer prices lead to peasants producing less for the market and thereby contribute to the agricultural crisis affecting most countries in sub-Saharan Africa (World Bank, 1981: p. 55).

What is important to note is that, no matter how much damage these poor policies do to African economies, they provide clear benefits to African leaders. Therefore, economic reform of these harmful policies will only occur when these same élites are provided with strong-enough incentives to change. Popular pressure by citizens hurt by poor economic policies is not enough to change government policies because the vast majority of African countries have political systems that do not require them to be responsive to the demands of the population. Indeed, most countries in Africa have suffered severe drops in their real per capita incomes over the past ten years but there have been very few protests that even indirectly threatened the state. The International Monetary Fund provides incentives to change poor policies because African countries must assure the Fund that they are making significant reforms before they can receive any further credit. Thus, African countries, albeit in a rather halting manner, have begun to make at least some reforms in the public sector, exchange-rate regimes, and agricultural policies.

Unfortunately, too many assume that African leaders simply have become aware of their mistakes, and are therefore changing their economies in order to do what is best for their country. For instance, the United Nations Advisory Group on Financial Flows for Africa (1988: p. 1) wrote of African countries' reform efforts, 'African governments . . . recognizing that in the past they had not always used the resources available to them in the most effective way . . . [reaffirmed] that domestic economic reforms were necessary'. However, this view seems naive given the political advantages that poor economic policies provide for African leaders. There is no evidence that most African élites have become convinced to actually reform policies that have helped them so much. As will be noted below, a belief that economic reforms in Africa are voluntary leads to mistakenly disassociating structural reform from debt relief.

The African Debt Problem

Given the magnitude of the debt problem in Africa, it is not surprising that many people recommend drastic measures that do not take into account recent efforts to reform economies. By 1986, African debt had increased by 186 per cent over the 1980 level (World Bank, 1988*c*: p. 6). Debt-service obligations are therefore extremely high. In 1986, African countries owed the equivalent of 45 per cent of the value of their exports. In 1987, that figure dropped to 36 per cent but the poorest African countries still had to pay 49 per cent of their exports in debt service. Indeed, because of the economic crisis affecting African states, not all of this debt is being paid. Actual debt service in 1986 was approximately 29 per cent and this figure decreased to 25 per cent in 1987. In all, only twelve African countries have serviced their debt since 1980 (UNDP and World Bank, 1989: p. 17). As Reginald Green (1986: p. 22) notes, current African debt levels are 'objectively unmanageable with existing terms, conditions, and export prospects'.

Even in African countries that have done relatively well over the last few years, debt has been a major problem. For instance, Ghana, the country that has probably gone the furthest in adopting economic-reform policies, has not made much progress on its debt problem as debt service as a percentage of goods and services exported has increased from 8.3 per cent in 1980 to 16.7 per cent in 1986 (World Bank, 1988*b*: p. 29). Indeed, structural adjustment of the type recommended by the World Bank is predicated on large new flows of finance being received by African countries, so even under the most optimistic scenarios there is no way that economic reforms by themselves can solve the African debt problem (World Bank, 1986).

There are two aspects of African debt which are important to note in designing a viable solution to the African debt problem. First, African debt is relatively small by world standards, amounting to only 10 per cent of total developing country debt (UNDP and World Bank, 1989: p. 18). Further, 25 per cent of total African debt is accounted for by Nigeria (World Bank, 1988*a* and 1988*c*) which, because of its size and the characteristics of its debt, is usually treated as a special case. Second, most African debt, unlike the debt of Latin American countries, is owed to official creditors, either other governments or multilateral organizations such as the International Monetary Fund and the World Bank. In 1986, official creditors and multilateral organizations accounted for approximately 69 per cent of total African debt while private creditors accounted for only 31 per cent of the debt (World Bank, 1988*b*: p. 6). In contrast, 25 per cent of Latin American debt is owed to official creditors (World Bank, 1988*b*: p. 18). There are only a few countries (Congo-Brazzaville, Côte d'Ivoire, Gabon, Nigeria, Zimbabwe) where debt to private creditors exceeds debt to official creditors (calculated from World Bank, 1988*a* and 1988*c*). Not surprisingly, these countries are among the wealthiest on the African continent and therefore among the few that are attractive to private creditors. African debt may be much more tractable than Latin American debt because the amounts are smaller and because western countries can take action directly rather than having to work through (and sometimes against) commercial banks.

Yet there has not been substantial movement on African debt because there is no institutional imperative for any organization to take into account the debt problem when proposing economic reforms for African countries. The International Monetary Fund is primarily interested in seeing that African countries resolve balance-of-payments problems and therefore concentrates mainly on proposals that reduce internal demand and that can be implemented in two to three years. Similarly, the World Bank has been involved mainly in project lending and has only recently been willing to lend money in order to fund structural reforms of African economies. There is, therefore, no direct link between the reforms actually carried out by African countries and the multilateral, bilateral, and private debt that they owe. As a result, even if African countries fully embrace the economic reforms suggested by outside authorities, there is no way at present to keep debt problems from still overwhelming them and destroying any hopes for growth.

Proposed Solutions for the African Debt Problem

There have been a large number of proposals to ameliorate the African debt problem. For instance, the UN Advisory Group on Financial Flows for Africa suggested a package of policies including turning official development loans into grants, rescheduling principal and interest for countries that cannot pay at all, generous terms and rescheduling of interest at below market rates, and additional funding from the World Bank and the IMF (United Nations Advisory Group on Financial Flows in Africa, 1988). Already, the major western countries have adopted a menu of concessions for especially poor countries that includes cancelling one-third of the debt, extending maturities, and providing concessional interest rates. Since these options were adopted at the 1988 Western Economic Summit, several countries have benefited including Mali, Central African Republic, Madagascar, Niger, and Tanzania. The International Monetary Fund estimates that if the menu approach was applied to the entire debt of a country, the present value of the debt could be reduced by up to 20 per cent. The IMF has also established facilities to aid countries on concessionary terms if they undertake structural reforms (International Monetary Fund, 1989: p. 103).

However, there are a significant number of problems with these proposals. First, they mainly apply to the poorest countries in Africa. As the UNDP and the World Bank noted in 1989 (p. 19), no strategy has yet been adopted for middle-income countries in Africa even though, as the case of Ghana illustrates, unless the debt problem is solved no amount of structural reform will allow even middle-income African countries to grow. In addition, these proposals do not address the problem of debt owed to multilateral organizations such as the World Bank. Approximately 34 per cent of the debt service actually paid by African countries in 1987 was to multilateral organizations (UNDP and World Bank, 1989: p. 18) and it is clear that the IMF and the World Bank will be the major sources of new loans to African countries in the future. In the case of Ghana, almost 83 per cent of the new debt that the country acquired between 1980 and 1987 came from multilateral donors (World Bank, 1988*c*: p. 26).

Most importantly, should these proposals alleviate the debt burden of even the poorest countries, there may be a very strong temptation on the part of African leaders to reduce the pace of economic reform. Indeed, even if the debt relief programs do not send the message directly that continued economic reform is unnecessary for aid from the outside, the precedent of Western countries unilaterally helping African countries without extracting the kind of elaborate promises that the International Monetary Fund requires before it provides funds may have a chilling effect on the motivation of many African leaders who have to make tough decisions if they are to have economic reform. This is an important point because, as noted above, it is extremely doubtful, given the political benefits of rampant state intervention in African economies, that leaders will voluntarily continue with economic reforms as assumed by the UN Advisory Group on Financial Flows and others who recommend debt relief without strings. There is, in fact, every reason to believe that without dramatic external pressure, poor economic policies in African countries will continue.

The problem stems once again from the fact that there is no direct link between structural reform and debt relief. Just as the International Monetary Fund demands economic relief but can do little about the debt problem which is strangling many African countries, the current crop of proposals for debt relief ignore structural reforms which are vital if African countries are ever going to grow. The solution is, therefore, to develop ways whereby continued economic reform is directly linked to debt relief.

Linking Economic Reform to Debt Relief

No one solution will be found to the debt problem. There are a few countries (for example Nigeria and Zimbabwe) which probably can follow the Latin American precedent of debt rescheduling, because a substantial portion of their debt is owed to private creditors. The link between economic reform and debt relief for these countries will be easily maintained because the countries will not get their debt rescheduled unless they adopt better economic policies. For the majority of African countries, however, Western governments and multilateral creditors will have to jointly adopt a set of policies that promises substantial debt relief while still providing incentives to African leaders to continue politically difficult economic reform. A combination of the following policies should be adopted in order to address all the economic concerns of African countries with the specific mix depending on individual circumstances.

First, *at least some official debt should be made payable in local currency to internationally administered funds for reinvestment in local economies.* Current debt payments require African countries to devote much of their limited hard currency to debt service and thereby prevents them from purchasing capital equipment and inputs desperately needed if business is to grow and to operate efficiently. However, if the debt was required to be paid into an internal account that went for reinvestment, then the economies of African countries would not be as starved for foreign funds.

Requiring governments to meet their debt obligations in local currency keeps the pressure on African governments to reform because almost all the debt is public and therefore must be repaid by African governments. They still have incentives to continue reforms that will make them operate more efficiently, especially by reforming public sector enterprises. At the same time, this proposal will help by reinvigorating the growth of the rest of the economy because vitally needed foreign exchange will no longer be diverted to debt payments.

The only danger is that countries might try to simply inflate out of their local currency obligations by printing more money. However, if the actual level of debt was still priced in US dollars, then there is no way that simply increasing the money supply would reduce the debt because increasing inflation would simply raise the nominal level of local currency debt without affecting real levels of debt.

There is also already quite a bit of experience on the part of international aid agencies in allocating local currency to industries and organizations that can utilize it productively. For instance, American embassies have developed large surpluses of local currency over the years from the sale of food aid and from commodity import programs. It would not be difficult to establish a series of internationally administered funds that would aid productive industries and organizations with the money that would have gone to debt service. Presumably, both economic enterprises and other organizations, such as non-governmental aid agencies, could receive these funds as long as they were proposing useful projects.

Second, *actual debt relief measures should be tied to countries meeting strict performance guidelines.* For instance, the western countries could agree that they would progressively forgive 30 per cent of an African country's official debt if the country held its real exchange rate in balance for five years. Since overvaluation is a major problem in many African countries, keeping the exchange rate at a level that would not cause economic distortion would be a major achievement. Further, African leaders would see that if they followed the agreed exchange rate policy, they would achieve real economic benefits rather than just accumulating more money that would have to be transferred to creditors. Alternatively, another creditor could agree to forgive part of an African country's debt if the government provided farmers with a high rate of income for an agreed period of time.

Under present regulations, the World Bank and the International Monetary Fund would not be able to participate in any plan to tie debt relief directly to structural reform because their by-laws require that they be paid back. Serious consideration should be given to changing these provisions or to having western countries make up the funds to the multilateral organizations if the regulations cannot be changed. As noted above, African debt (especially once Nigeria is removed) is not large in absolute terms, and the multilateral organizations would therefore not be significantly hurt if they did not receive some payments from some African countries for part of the debt the poor states owe. Indeed, given the debt crisis that most African countries face, the multilateral organizations probably will not be paid back in any event and the question then becomes whether debt relief can be done on a systematic basis that still provides incentives for economic reform or whether debt relief is to be done on an *ad hoc* basis in a crisis atmosphere where countries suspend debt payments *and* economic reform.

Third, *new money should be devoted to aiding African economies, but that new money should be predicated on programs of economic reform*. In addition to some outright debt relief, African countries will need new financial flows if countries are to grow out of their economic problems. Already, the United States has adopted a new program which devotes more money to African countries that have adopted specific economic reforms. However, this program receives only $75 million a year (Donatelli, 1984: p. 7), hardly enough to make an impact on the African debt problem. If the US and other countries are able to devote more money to Africa, these funds should be made explicitly contingent on countries concluding economic reform. Further, more attention should be given to generous funding of the World Bank so that it can provide more funds at concessional rates to African countries that are pursuing economic reform.

Conclusion

There will eventually be debt relief in Africa. The debt levels are simply too high to be serviceable and more and more African leaders will probably begin to refuse to pay back debts given the economic depression that most countries have been in for the last fifteen years. The goal of Western policy toward Africa should, therefore, be to design a set of economic policies which addresses the debt problem but still forces African leaders to make economic reforms that they probably do not want to implement. This type of policy is much more difficult than others simply demanding different reforms or unilaterally granting debt relief. African countries and the major donors will have to choreograph an intricate minuet where, in an atmosphere of increasing trust, tough decisions on economic reform are met by increasingly generous debt-reduction measures. Certainly, nothing could be worse than debt relief which allows African leaders to go back to following poor economic policies with regard to public-sector enterprises, the exchange-rate regime, and agriculture. Such a result would mean that African economies would continue to stagnate and Western countries would probably be discouraged from ever again trying to aid African countries.

References

d'Almeida, Ayité-Fily (1986), 'La Privatisation des enterprises publiques en Afrique au sud du Sahara—Première Partie', *Le Mois en Afrique*, no. 245-6.

Anderson, Dennis (1987), *The Public Revenue and Economic Policy in African Countries*, World Bank Discussion Paper no. 19 (Washington, DC: The World Bank).

Bates, Robert H. (1981), *Markets and States in Tropical Africa* (Berkeley: University of California Press).

Commission of Inquiry into the Affairs of Certain Statutory Corporations in Western Nigeria (Coker Commission) (1962), *Report of Coker Commission of Inquiry into the Affairs of Certain Statutory Corporations in Western Nigeria*, vol. 1 (Lagos: Federal Ministry of Information).

Constantin, F. *et al.* (1979), *Les Enterprises Publiques en Afrique Noire*, vol. 1 (Paris: Centre d'Étude d'Afrique Noire).

Donatelli, Frank J. (1984), 'Statement of Frank J. Donatelli', *Economic*

Policy Initiative for Africa, US Congress Committee on Foreign Affairs Hearing, ninety-eighth congress, second session, 7 February.

Dutheil de la Rochère, Jacqueline (1976), *L'État de la Développement Économique de la Côte d'Ivoire* (Paris: Centre d'Étude d'Afrique Noire).

Green, Reginald Herbold (1986), 'Comments', in Carol Lancaster and John Williamson (eds.), *African Debt and Financing* (Washington, DC: Institute for International Economics).

Hyden, Goran (1983), *No Shortcuts to Progress* (Berkeley: University of California).

International Monetary Fund (1989), 'Paris Club Implements Menu Approach for Low Income Countries', *IMF Survey*, 3 April.

Nellis, John R. (1986), *Public Enterprises in Sub-Saharan Africa*, World Bank Discussion Paper no. 1 (Washington, DC: World Bank).

Rondinelli, Dennis A., John R. Nellis, and G. Shabbir Cheema (1984), *Decentralization in Developing Countries*, World Bank Staff Working Paper no. 581 (Washington, DC: World Bank).

Short, R. P. (1984), 'The Role of Public Enterprises: An International Statistical Comparison', in Robert H. Floyd *et al.*, *Public Enterprises in Mixed Economies* (Washington, DC: International Monetary Fund).

United Nations Advisory Group on Financial Flows for Africa (1988), *Financing Africa's Recovery* (NY: United Nations).

United Nations Development Program and the World Bank (1989), *Africa's Adjustment and Growth in the 1980s* (Washington, DC: The World Bank).

World Bank (1981), *Accelerated Development in Sub-Saharan Africa* (Washington, DC: The World Bank).

—— (1986), *Financing Adjustment with Growth in Sub-Saharan Africa, 1986–1990* (Washington, DC: The World Bank).

—— (1988*a*), *World Debt Tables* (Washington, DC: The World Bank).

—— (1988*b*), *World Debt Tables*, first supplement (Washington, DC: The World Bank).

—— (1988*c*), *World Debt Tables*, second supplement (Washington, DC: The World Bank).

Stock Markets and the Balance of Economic and Political Reform in the People's Republic of China

SPECIAL MERIT AWARD

Editors' Introduction

In this essay Davin Mackenzie of Strategic Planning Associates explores the difficulties facing the process of economic reform in China in general, by using the development of stock markets as a 'vehicle for this analysis'. The history and current position of the country's stock markets, which take up much of the essay, should be seen as *one* important element in reform; there are many other factors which are more important. The development of stock markets does however, concentrate many of the contentious issues facing economic and political reform. In many ways they are the embodiment of capitalism and therefore are at risk politically. The author also argues that there are many legal barriers to the Chinese stock markets developing further. He also argues that the inability of the stock market to develop fully means that it does not serve the purpose of channelling savings into profitable investments, so although China has succeeded in raising savings rates, this is not reflected in good investments.

Davin A. Mackenzie, 29, is an Associate with Strategic Planning Associates, an international corporate strategy and management consulting firm headquartered in Washington, D.C.. Previously he worked for the Bank of Boston in Taipei, Taiwan as a corporate-finance specialist. He has lived in mainland China and Taiwan for over five years, including a year as a student at Beijing Normal University, and is a fluent Mandarin speaker. He is a recent Masters graduate of the Lauder Institute of Management and International Studies at the Wharton School and the University of Pennsylvania and a previous graduate of Dartmouth College.

10

Stock Markets and the Balance of Economic and Political Reform in the People's Republic of China

DAVIN A. MACKENZIE

1. Introduction

Westerners are fascinated by the recent political and economic reforms being undertaken in China and the Soviet Union. In a sense we are flattered by the degree to which these two countries adopt capitalistic and democratic ways that resemble our own. That the PRC and the USSR are experiencing great internal stress as a result of these reforms comes as little surprise. However, media reports have not emphasized the degree to which reform has undermined the very basis of decades of political and economic orthodoxy, especially in China. It is the purpose of this essay to explore the problems associated with transforming a socialist economy into a more market-oriented economy. As a vehicle for this analysis this essay will concentrate on the development of stock markets in China. While stock market experiments in the PRC are not the most important of their reforms, they are interesting due to their sophisticated nature and the degree to which their development concentrates all the contentious issues associated with economic and political reform.

Recent accounts of the growing role of stock markets in China give the misleading impression that they are an integral part of the Chinese economy. What is not explained is the enormous amount of reform in the most basic aspects of economic structure that needs to be done before stock markets in China can function effectively and contribute to the development of the economy. This essay's central thesis is that the political, economic, legal, and institutional conditions for the proper functioning of stock markets do not now exist in China and that therefore the introduction of stock markets now is both economically premature and politically vulnerable.

2. China's Economic Reforms

From 1958 until 1978 China had a centrally managed command economy characterized by 1) national ownership of all means of production and their organization into vertical systems of administrative controls, 2) a strong egalitarian ethic, and 3) relative isolation from the outside world.[1] State-owned industrial enterprises operated according to a 'material balances' system where each enterprise's inputs and outputs were planned and were supposed to match perfectly. Enterprises were given annual budgets from the government and had to remit back profits but were not held responsible for deficits as it was all considered part of one 'big pot'.

The financial sector consisted of one bank that acted as the cashier for the government planning mechanisms.[2] Money was just an accounting unit. Enterprises were the focus of each worker's social security benefits such as housing, rations, medical care, and so on. Jobs were tenured lifetime positions, and the term 'iron rice bowls' describes the permanence of the benefits.

Enterprises were motivated to maximize employee benefits and resources under their control, not profits. Enterprises therefore had constant demand for financing, hence the term 'investment hunger'. That these investment funds were provided interest free by the government made investment even more attractive. As a result, growth prior to 1979 was characterized by high rates of investment and poor and constantly declining factor productivity.[3]

Until 1978 all state-owned enterprises and collectives were under the complete control of Communist Party cadres who were concerned not with profits but with political objectives and administration of government directives.[4]

Following the death of Mao Zedong and the end of the Cultural Revolution in 1976 the Chinese economy was in a shambles. Deng Xiaoping came to power and took advantage of a national desire for change. China began a massive program of economic reform in 1978, the bulk of which originally concentrated on the agricultural sector. In 1984 the emphasis turned to the industrial sector. The reforms are characterized by three major themes, 1) greater decentralization of microeconomic decision making, 2) increased reliance on the market function and material incentives, and 3) gradual opening of the economy to the outside world. To carry out this transformation two fundamental changes in the old system were needed: first, separation of enterprise management from government control, and emphasis on profit rather than size maximization. Second, a shift of responsibility for investment financing from the government to the enterprise through the development of a commercially oriented financial intermediation sector. Enterprises were allowed to keep a share of their profits and the formation of collectives and individually owned businesses was encouraged.[5]

Investment decisions were to be based on the principle of profit maximization and bottomline responsibility for losses by both the enterprise and the financing institution. The banking sector was reorganized into a number of specialist institutions.

As part of the reform of banking and finance and the replacement of administrative by financial controls, the government intended to rely on credit, interest rates, and taxation to manipulate the economy.[6] Interest rates were raised to encourage savings. However, the effectiveness of the interest rate as an allocative mechanism was seriously hampered by one major conceptual problem; lenders did not have to evaluate credit risk, nor did borrowers have to assess the risk of high leverage and interest expense burden because the government did not allow enterprises to fail. The whole economy functioned on the idea that borrowers were either explicitly or implicitly guaranteed by the government. Banks just assumed the former distributive function of the government. Higher interest rates have done little to slow borrowing or increase its efficient use. The net result has been rampant money supply growth and inflation.[7]

China's annual average GNP growth of 9.98 per cent since 1981 makes it the world's fastest-growing economy. However, industrial growth has outstripped infrastructural growth. New investment is not being attracted to infrastructural projects that have irrationally low prices and long pay-backs. Old, inefficient industries are able to invest heavily and squander precious resources because they are still not allowed to fail. Inflation climbed from 7.3 per cent in 1987 to 18 per cent in 1988, with an early 1989 pace of around 25 per cent. In the face of resource constraints, infrastructural bottlenecks, continued high rates of investment, and the ineffectiveness of new indirect credit and interest rate tools, the government reverted to its old command style by ordering the halt of tens of thousands of projects.[8] The problems of the past two years illustrate the dramatic structural change that has occurred within China since 1978. As Robert Delfs observes:

The increasing complexity of emerging commercial and financial networks has outstripped the capacity of state financial and economic planners to even monitor and understand—much less manage—China's fast-changing economy. These changes make it doubtful that restoring order by simply rebuilding the old command-planning mechanisms will be economically or politically feasible.[9]

Economic reforms have unquestionably produced many positive results for China in the past ten years. But they have also caused many problems that call for further reform.

3. Economic and Legal Barriers to Further Reform

Economic reform in China will only succeed if the proper infrastructure is put in place to support it. In short, China must institute the basic fundamentals of a capitalist society such as bankruptcy laws, free labour markets, efficient pricing, and other elements of Western economies that we take for granted.

If the notion that bankruptcy as a discipline for inefficient enterprises is to be accepted then explicit laws must be established and precedents set. China is now drafting bankruptcy laws and a few firms in Shenyang have actually been allowed to go under.[10]

One of the biggest problems associated with increased enterprise efficiency and the allowance of bankruptcy is the difficulty in breaking the 'iron rice bowl' concept. This is problematic in a socialist country where two generations of urban workers have become accustomed to cradle-to-grave welfare certainty. It is estimated that about 15 per cent of the urban workforce, or 20 million people, is redundant. Part of the recent economic reforms is aimed at breaking the iron rice bowl by replacing it with a 'labour contract system' whereby workers would have negotiated contracts with their employers and would be subject to dismissal for poor performance. The other side of this reform is that workers would then have some freedom to choose their own work instead of being assigned to work-units without choice. However, it should not be assumed that all economic reforms, no matter how good for the economy as a whole, are universally popular. There is much opposition to this kind of reform amongst both managers and workers as it represents a substantial break with past comfortable habits.[11]

Another barrier to economic reform of every kind in China is the centrally planned pricing system. Until 1978 virtually all prices were set by the central government, often without reference to production costs or market conditions. When prices are not allowed to perform their equilibrating function in an economy serious distortions result. For example, because petroleum products were priced at 70-80 per cent below world market prices, not only was excessive use encouraged but increased production was discouraged. There is a constant shortage of high quality and a plethora of low-quality goods. Moreover, since firms cannot control their prices, profits are not a reflection of their performance. Enterprises' incentives are not to improve operations but instead to manœuvre politically with their supervisory organizations. Since 1978 there has been some limited price reform with the introduction of the two-tier system whereby enterprises contract with the state for certain quantities at set prices, but any extra production can be sold as they wish for whatever prices the market will bear. This has had limited effect in equilibrating markets.[12] Price reform has to be taken to its logical extreme and prices, with a few strategic exceptions, left to the market to decide. This is necessary so that enterprises' profits reflect their performance and so that investment can be allocated more efficiently to those areas of the economy where demand is greatest.

China's accounting standards are primitive and lack uniformity. Financial accounting needs to be improved so that outsiders can more easily evaluate firm risk and so that enterprise managers can more efficiently run their businesses. Moreover, financial and market information needs to be widely distributed. In a country where access to information is a function of political rank and even the most banal information is classified as government secrets this entrenched attitude will be difficult to break. Without accurate and timely information an efficient economy is impossible.

Enterprise tax policies need to be overhauled. For example, enterprises are allowed to deduct interest *and principal* repayment

for tax purposes.[13] This drastically reduces the cost of debt,
therefore encouraging its indiscriminate use and making other
means of finance such as equity much less attractive.

The lack of a coherent set of laws and regulations governing a
more market-oriented economy is a major obstacle to economic
reform in China. It has been estimated that 70 per cent of China's
laws would need to be rewritten in order to conform to a more
market-oriented economy.[14]

4. On the Theory of Financial Liberalization

Chinese economic reform is proceeding on many fronts: in agriculture, foreign trade, industry, and in finance. In the financial
sector the reforms and changes resemble in important ways the
major policies recommended by the 'financial liberalization' or
'financial deepening' school of economic development. In important
other ways China's changes differ radically.

The financial liberalization school of economic development came
to prominence in the late 1960s and early 1970s through the writings
of Goldsmith, Shaw, and McKinnon. The basic hypotheses are
that there is a historically observable direct relationship between
the financial development of a country and its economic growth.
The financial development of a country is measured by the size of its
total financial assets relative to either national wealth (Goldsmith's
definition of the financial interrelations ratio or FIR) or GNP
(Shaw's definition of financial depth). Proponents argue that
financial development is therefore an engine for economic growth
in developing countries, and to these theorists such financial
development necessarily involves the withdrawal of government
intervention in the financial sector, the removal of ceilings on
interest rates, and the unfettered existence of uncertainty or risk.[15]
The theory of financial liberalization is that unrestricted (and
presumably higher) interest rates will produce a permanent increase
in saving and therefore in investment. The higher cost of investment
will divert it from less productive uses. As McKinnon says:

. . . high rates of interest for both lenders and borrowers introduce the
dynamism that one wants in development, calling forth net savings and
diverting investments from inferior uses so as to encourage technical
improvement. In contrast, the common policy of maintaining low or

negative rates of interest on financial assets and limited loan availability may accomplish neither.[16]

Theoretically, the differential risk of failure of every project or enterprise leads to a differentiated pricing in terms of interest rates, and therefore an ability to allocate investment more efficiently.

In response to higher nominal interest rates and large increases in income, financial savings have grown dramatically in China in the last ten years. China now has one of the highest savings rates in the world. Between 1978 and 1985 savings grew at an average annual pace of 28.9 per cent, compared to 10.6 per cent for the twenty-five previous years. China's savings rate now is approximately 32-6 per cent of GDP, comparable to Japan and the East Asian NICs.[17]

This strong saving rate contributes to the relatively high 'depth' of China's financial sector compared to many other developing countries, with a ratio of financial assets to GNP of 100 per cent in 1984 versus 80 per cent for India, 108 per cent for Brazil or 176 per cent for the United States. The composition of this depth reflects the primitive nature of China's financial sector in that virtually all of the financial assets are held by banks, with insurance companies, finance companies, and investment funds virtually nonexistent.[18]

China's economic reforms are engendering great difficulties because, while they have created the conditions for greater financial depth, they have not allowed the creation of policies and institutions that are necessary for the second part of the financial liberalization equation. The theory of financial liberalization relies on the raising of the interest rate to allocate the increased savings to investment in a more efficient manner. Higher interest rates will make poor investment projects unprofitable and risky to undertake. There is still little downside risk to investment in China. There are no bankruptcy costs. The price of investment to the borrower is meaningless and investment hunger continues unabated. In order for financial liberalization to succeed, the concept of risk and bankruptcy must be introduced into the economy so that investment will be allocated more efficiently.

5. The History of Stock Markets in the PRC

There was a stock market in Shanghai between 1919 and 1949. It was not a significant source of financing for enterprises, was highly speculative, and dominated by a few rich individuals.[19]

The first appearances of stocks in China since 1949 occurred in 1984 when collective enterprises, not being able to satisfy their investment hunger with rationed bank credit, started issuing 'shares' to employees in exchange for funds.[20] By early 1989 over 6,000 enterprises, including a few state-owned firms, had issued 'shares' worth almost US $6 billion. A few even had their shares trade publicly on stock exchanges that were developed in Shanghai, Shenyang, Wuhan, and Chongqing.[21]

The original 'shares' were shares in name only and actually more closely resembled bonds. Most of the original 'shares' had a short maturity, a high minimum guaranteed yield, and the possibility of a higher bonus yield in case of good enterprise performance. But they had no voting or shareholder rights nor any claim on the equity of the firm, and had restrictions on transferability. For many enterprises the share system was a disguised method for issuing more bonuses to workers, with a dividend yield of 30 per cent being normal and some enterprises even paying 100 per cent. In response the People's Bank of China (the central bank and regulatory authority) limited payouts on such 'share' instruments to 15 per cent per annum.[22]

By 1985 'share' issues had become immensely popular, though still only used by collectives and individual enterprises (state-owned enterprises were not allowed to issue shares at this stage) and mostly issued to employees. In 1984–5 there were 2,000 new issues in Shanghai with a total value of ¥200 million (US $67 million), in Guangdong 330 issues worth US $167 million, and Jiangsu accounted for US $700 million. However, these amounts were small compared to other sources of enterprise finance. In 1985 total enterprise loans by Chinese banks alone (excluding government grant funds) totalled US $179 billion.[23]

So far most 'shares' have been issued by collectives directly to their own workers and staff. While there have been problems with excess payouts, there have also been many examples of major improvements in the operation of enterprises once its workers are given a stake. Despite forty years of 'ownership by the people', it is only when the workers have a direct individual stake that they believe that the enterprise truly belongs to them. In Marxist jargon, 'the property relations of the enterprise have been put in order'.[24] This type of incentive scheme is an integral part of China's economic reforms.

Experiments with the 'share' system have produced many innovations. Some have arisen in an uncontrolled manner out of individual enterprise needs, some have been explicitly sanctioned by the government. An example of the former is the Yanzhong Industrial Company of Shanghai, a collective firm with 4,000 employees. In 1985 it offered 100,000 shares for sale to the general public. Demand was high, 18,000 individuals purchased shares, and the offering sold out within a half-day. The pay-out for the stock was 7.2 per cent guaranteed, 15 per cent maximum. The Yanzhong share issue had two main innovations; first, it was made available to the general public, not just employees (in fact Yanzhong workers bought less than 10 per cent of the issue), and second, it gave limited shareholder-voting rights to the purchasers. The principal responsibility of the shareholder is to elect the board of directors at an annual meeting of stockholders' representatives. This innovation was limited, however, in that Yanzhong's management decides who the 'stockholders' representatives' will be.

None the less, this type of innovation is critical in trying to introduce a separation of ownership and management in Chinese enterprises as well as instilling a sense of management-accountability to interests other than the government.[25]

Other innovations have taken on a more idiosyncratic Chinese nature. In order to increase the appeal of 'share' issues, some firms have taken advantage of the Chinese penchant for gambling by offering investors the choice between a low 2 per cent dividend with participation in a lottery for large cash prizes, and a regular 9 per cent dividend with no lottery feature. Still others have offered pay-outs in scarce consumer goods. One bond issue in the petrochemical sector offered buyers priority-allocation of the project's output.[26]

In 1986 the government allowed limited 'share' issuing experiments in the state-owned enterprise sector. The most profound experiment has been with the Gold Cup Automobile Company of Shenyang.[27] In July 1988 Gold Cup issued US $26.9 million of stock to the public, the largest issue in China to date. Gold Cup is now explicitly owned 50 per cent by the state, 40 per cent by designated companies, 7 per cent by corporate investors, and 3 per cent by individuals. It is the largest company in China to issue stock, and its shares are theoretically for sale to any citizen. Also in theory, shareholders have the right to vote on management selection. Gold Cup also has a diverse board of directors made up of experts in law, economics, and history rather than only Communist Party officials. The explicit objective is to separate government from management. And finally, Gold Cup's shares are listed on the Shenyang stock market.

China's stock-markets are small, primitive, and relatively inactive. Of 6,000 enterprises that have issued 'shares' since 1984, only fourteen have sold to the public.[28] Of these publicly purchased shares, only 3 per cent have been traded. Only nine out of the fourteen enterprises have seen any trading in their sstock. Shanghai's stock exchange is the largest with six firms listed. Shenyang's sole listed firm is Gold Cup. The Wuhan and Chongqing markets have little to no trading.

The Shanghai market opened in September 1986.[29] Initially there was virtually no activity because there were no sellers. Weeks would go by without trading and prices never changed. Chinese purchasers, being inexperienced and cautious, are looking for high dividend yield rather than capital gain and thus have little incentive to trade. Volume now on the Shanghai market is about 1,500 shares a week with prices apparently allowed to float freely.[30] Prices do change slightly, with occasional decreases, but in general prices only go up and there is little perception of risk. Gold Cup stock has yet to trade in Shenyang.

The early experiments quickly revealed two fundamental conceptual problems that remain to be resolved. The first is that of risk, the second concerns a proper definition of equity. In the West, shares in a company embody a certain risk, generally greater than in the same company's bonds, for which the holder is to be compensated with slightly higher return. The risk-return trade-off is a fundamental equation in investment decision-making. However, this is not true for Chinese 'shares'. First, the rate of return on the 'shares' has little correlation with enterprise performance. On the one hand investors get a minimum return no matter how poorly the enterprise does, but on the other hand the maximum upside return is bounded, even if the riskiness of the venture warrants a higher return.[31] Second, the principal is also essentially guaranteed. Therefore the 'shares' have virtually no risk.

The combination of socialist history and a primitive financial sector have led to serious problems in differentiating between equity and debt. In theory, equity is money provided by the 'owners' of the firm that entitles them to a claim on the residual value of the firm's assets and its income flows. In small or individually owned enterprises in China this equity is explicitly contributed by the entrepreneur. In the larger collective and state-owned enterprises there is no explicit base of funds defined as equity or as belonging to the 'owners'. Neither the accounting nor the legal framework of Chinese business is equipped properly to define equity and its rights and limitations.[32] Since stock markets by definition are for the trading of equity securities, the lack of appropriate frameworks is a serious barrier to wider use of stocks by enterprises.

Until the uncertainties about the legal basis of the shareholding system are resolved, most companies, unless explicitly sanctioned by the government, are not likely to fully exploit the advantages of issuing shares, and therefore a strong stock market is not likely to evolve.

In addition to all the above general economic barriers there are many securities market-specific institutions that need to be nurtured in order to have functioning stock markets. For example, China will need to develop accounting and auditing firms, investment funds, credit agencies, stock analysts, corporate lawyers, brokers, dealers, enforcement agencies, and the like. As China transforms itself from a centrally planned command economy into a decentralized market economy nothing can be taken for granted, and infrastructure and customs need to be explicitly instituted before anything as sophisticated as a stock market can be expected to function effectively.

The primitive nature of China's stock markets is a reflection of their experimental nature, public lack of understanding, the absence of any unifying underlying regulation or structure, as well as a short supply of stocks. While revolutionary compared to what was thought possible ten years ago, it is not clear that stock-markets are here to stay in China. There is the fact that 6,000 enterprises have issued close to US $6 billion of stocks and bonds to employees and the public and that many economists are calling for total privatization of the economy.[33] At the same time, the Chinese economy is experiencing problems, a good part of the proceeds of the issues have been squandered on unproductive investments or inflationary bonuses, and there is considerable ideological and political opposition. In February 1989 the government announced it was freezing further experiments with shareholding systems in state-owned enterprises. This was to control inflation by restricting spending and investment, to appease ideological conservatives that oppose the experiments, and to give the government time to come up with coherent policies for the experiments that so far have proceeded in an uncoordinated and unregulated fashion.[34]

6. Political Barriers to Stock Market Development

Since the Tiananmen massacre and the retrenchment of conservative power within the Communist Party there has been a significant reversal in the momentum that previous economic reforms had brought into the political debate on the future nature of China's system. It is unclear whether the various localized repressions of entrepreneurial activity and other reforms, such as share issues, will become more widespread or official. It is notable, however, that there has yet to be any official reversal of the most important directions of the reform: separation of management and government, and the increased privatization of the economy. There are many divergent opinions on the desirable extent of these reforms and this debate provides insights into just how threatening the economic reforms had become politically.

A major objective of economic reform is to rid enterprise management of the burden of excess government interference. In 1986 new policies explicitly dethroned the Communist Party from enterprise management and put the managers themselves in charge of everything. This is called the Factory Director Responsibility System.[35] The results of this change have been mixed,with many Party cadres firmly resisting the downgrading of their importance. As Plasschaert observes: 'Changes in economic systemic rules unavoidably affect the relative power positions of the organs and persons involved. Those whose decision making powers are curtailed are likely to oppose the moves.'[36] Enterprise managers need to be free to make decisions if they are going to be held accountable for profits instead of the achievement of government objectives. This highlights the degree to which, as Chamberlain says, 'economic reforms can only proceed on the basis of more exhaustive political reforms'.[37]

The most interesting political issue concerns the ideological debate surrounding the shareholding experiments. Some young Chinese economists have advocated that all state-owned firms be sold directly to the public and operate much like large US corporations. The young economists (Hua Sheng, Zhang Xuejun, Luo Xiaopeng) are all academics and represent the most extreme position within the establishment debate. They believe that only with the reintroduction of full individual private property rights will price and enterprise reform function effectively. Basically they want the complete removal of the government and Party from the economy. Under their scheme, the Party and bureaucracy's resistance would be overcome by buying their co-operation by giving them a larger share of the state's assets when they are distributed to the public.[38]

On the other extreme, more traditional socialist economists have viciously and ceaselessly attacked the shareholding experiments and the young economists' proposals as total anathema to Marxism. Indeed, the shareholding ideas and stock market experiments are a complete break with traditional Marxist–Leninist thought and socialist economics. As Ma and Hong put it: 'if these ideas are put into practice, the road to communism will be blocked. The *Manifesto of the Communist Party* says that the purpose of communism is to eliminate capitalist private ownership of the means of production and eliminate the system of man exploiting man. Private ownership runs counter to communism; it certainly does not apply to the actual conditions of China.'[39]

A sort of middle-ground has emerged from this debate that advocates the conversion of the government's role from an administrative director of enterprises to a role more akin to an institutional investor. One economist, Xu Jing'an, advocates that the government manage state assets through the formation of holding companies that would in turn invest in enterprises. The holding company's primary, if not sole objective would be to maximize profits. The holding companies, given a limited budget, would be forced to allocate their investments to enterprises that promised the highest return. The enterprises, dependent on the holding company investment for survival, would be forced to act in a more efficient manner. In theory this system would combine the best of capitalist motivation and state ownership.[40] How this would effect individual worker motivation and whether there would be a role for individual ownership, even if only for employees, is not clear. Whether such a system would even need a stock market is even less clear, although its best promise would probably be in providing a transitional stage from the present system to one based on individual ownership.

It is impossible to separate politics from economics when it comes to reform. Progress in one area inevitably leads to demand for change in the other. In China's case economics preceded politics. It is interesting that the Soviet Union's course is exactly opposite. As economic reforms gave individuals greater freedom to determine their own economic fate without Party direction or control, it lessened the importance of the Party in people's lives.

The danger lies in trying to push for too sharp a break with the past and with the ideological foundation of the Communist Party. The history of the PRC is replete with examples of dramatic advances and then more dramatic retreats and repressions. Therefore stock-markets, as an extreme manifestation of an economic reform that has surged ahead of the political reforms that would be consistent with them, are extremely vulnerable politically. The long-run benefits of having stock-markets as a tool for financial development are substantial. Therefore China would be advised to downplay stock market experimentation in the short term, because any strong political attack on them now might deeply repress them and jeopardize their ability to reappear when the proper conditions for their function might exist.

Postscript

This essay was largely written before the Tiananmen massacre and the consolidation of conservative power within the Chinese Communist Party. After first thinking that these events had made my discussion of stock markets seem trivial and irrelevant I decided that if anything my essay underscores the delicate nature of political and economic reform and can perhaps aid people in understanding the difficulty of radically changing an embedded system. Tragically, the young proponents of political reform paid the ultimate price in pursuit of their ideals and it is to their memory that this essay is dedicated.

Notes

[1] The PRC was founded in 1949. The period from 1949 to 1958 can be characterized as the rebuilding and reorganization of the Chinese economy.

2 World Bank (1988), p. 245; Zhou and Zhu (1988).

3 World Bank (1988), pp. 4-5.

4 Chamberlain (1987).

5 Collectives means co-operatively owned. Sometimes they are made up of groups of individuals but mostly they are composed of groups of companies or government entities. Collectives were very important during the 1950s and 1960s, but by the 1970s had largely disappeared. World Bank (1988), p. 8.

6 De Wulf (1985).

7 World Bank (1988), p. 11; Fei and Reynolds (1988).

8 Delfs (1989*b*, 1989*c*); do Rosario (1989*a*, 1989*c*).

9 Delfs (1989*c*).

10 Chang (1987); Delfs (1989*b*); Kristoff (1989*a*).

11 White (1987).

12 Belassa (1988).

13 World Bank (1988), p. 123.

14 Karsten (1988).

15 McKinnon (1973), pp. 8-19; Drake (1980), pp. 25-30.

16 McKinnon (1973), p. 15.

17 EIU (1988); World Bank (1988), p. 27.

18 World Bank (1988), pp. 236-8.

19 Tamagna (1942); Young (1971).

20 Xu (1988).

21 Salem (1989).

22 World Bank (1988), p. 317; Xu (1988).

23 World Bank (1988), pp. 262, 317, and 319.

24 Xu (1985).

25 World Bank (1988), p. 127.

26 Grieves; Goodstadt (1987).

27 Kristoff (1989*a*).

28 To give further perspective on how low this activity is, the 6,000 enterprises represent just 1.3 per cent of the total of 463,200 collective and state-owned enterprises that existed in China as of the end of 1985; EIU (1988).

29 do Rosario (1989*d*).

30 Rowley (1989); Kristoff (1989*b*.)

31 Xu (1988).

32 World Bank (1988), pp. 142-3.

33 Delfs (1988).

34 Salem (1989).

35 Chamberlain (1987).

36 Plasschaert (1988).

37 Chamberlain (1987).

Davin Mackenzie

[38] Delfs (1988).
[39] Ma and Hong (1988).
[40] Xu (1988).

References

Balassa, Bela (1988), 'China's Economic Reforms in a Comparative Perspective ', in *Chinese Economic Reform: How Far, How Fast? (CER)* (Boston: Academic Press).

Chamberlain, Heath B. (1987), 'Party-Management Relations in Chinese Industries: Some Political Dimensions of Economic Reform', *The China Quarterly*, no. 112 (December).

Chang, Ta-Kuang (1987), 'The East is in the Red', *The China Business Review* (March–April), pp. 42–5.

Cho, Yoon Je (1986), 'Inefficiencies from Financial Liberalization in the Absence of Well-Functioning Equity Markets', *Journal of Money, Credit, and Banking* (May), pp. 191–9.

De Wulf, Luc (1985), 'Financial reform in China', *Finance & Development* (December), pp. 19–22.

Delfs, Robert (1988), 'Property to the people', *Far Eastern Economic Review (FEER)*, 12/22, pp. 12–13.

—— (1989a), 'The iron rice bowl cracks', *FEER*, 1/19, pp. 63–4.

—— (1989b), 'The perils of progress', *FEER*, 3/2, pp. 43–8.

—— (1989c), 'Tighten your belts', *FEER*, 3/30, pp. 10–11.

do Rosario, Louise (1989a), 'Peking's growing pains', *FEER*, 1/5, pp. 54–5.

—— (1989b), 'More swings than roundabouts', *FEER*, 3/2, pp. 48–9.

—— (1989c), 'Growth faces many hurdles', *FEER*, 3/2, pp. 49–50.

—— (1989d), 'Discounting the market', *FEER*, 3/9, p. 73.

Drake, P. J. (1980), *Money, Finance and Development* (New York: Hasted Press).

The Economist Intelligence Unit (EIU) (1988), *Country Profile: China, North Korea, 1988–89* (August).

EIU (1989), *Country Report: China, North Korea, No. 1, 1989*, 2/17.

Engle, Tom (1986), 'Stocks: New Domestic Financial Tool', *The China Business Review* (January–February), pp. 35–8.

Fei, John and Reynolds, Bruce (1988), 'A Tentative Plan for the

Rational Sequencing of Overall Reform in China's Economic System', in *CER*, pp. 490–520.

Goldsmith, Raymond W. (1969) *Financial Structure and Development* (New Haven: Yale University Press).

Goodstadt, Leo (1987), 'Bankers Learning to Trust Money', *Euromoney* (October), pp. 145–8.

Grieves, Robert (1986), 'Dynamic duo venture into capital business', *Asian Business* (October).

—— (1987), 'Economic reforms given a trial run in interior city', *Asian Business* (January), pp. 42–4.

Karsten, Siegfried G. (1988), 'China's Approach to Social Market Economics', *The American Journal of Economics and Sociology*, vol. 47, no. 2 (April).

Kristoff, Nicholas D. (1989a), 'Shenyang Showcase', *The New York Times* (26 February).

—— (1989b), 'Stock Markets' Role Grows in Chinese Economy', *The New York Times* (10 April).

Lee, Peter Nan-shong (1986), 'Enterprise Autonomy Policy in Post-Mao China: A Case Study of Policy-making, 1978–1983', *The China Quarterly*, no. 105 (March).

Leung, Julia (1989), 'China Faces Huge Ideological Hurdles in Plan to Sell Shares in State Concerns', *The Wall Street Journal* (January).

Ma Bin and Hong Zhunyan (1988). 'Enlivening Large State Enterprises: Where is the Motive Force?', in *CER*, pp. 503–8.

McKinnon, Ronald I. (1973), *Money and Capital in Economic Development* (Washington DC: The Brookings Institution).

Plasschaert, S.R. (1988), 'The Changing Role of Financial Management in State Enterprises in China', *MIR*, vol. 28, pp. 10–25.

Rong Wenzuo (1987), 'Establishing Joint Stock Companies: A Report of a Study on the Joint Development Company of the China Tourism Souvenirs Enterprise', *Chinese Economic Studies*, vol. 20, no. 3 (Spring).

Rowley, Anthony (1989), 'Market makers', *FEER*, 2/16, p. 48.

Salem, Ellen (1989), 'Peking ducks the issue', *FEER*, 3/9, p. 72.

Shaw, Edward S. (1973), *Financial Deepening in Economic Development* (New York: Oxford University Press).

Sudweeks, Bryan L. (1987) *Equity Market Development in Developing Countries: General Principles, Case Studies, Portfolio Implications, and Relevance to the People's Republic of China*, unpublished Ph.D. dissertation, School of Government and Business Administration, The George Washington University (March).

Tam, On-Kit (1988), 'Rural Finance in China', *The China Quarterly*, (March), pp. 60–76.

Tamagna, Frank M. (1942), *Banking and Finance in China* (New York: Institute of Pacific Relations).

Tidrich, Gene and Chen Jiyuan (1987) (eds.), *China's Industrial Reform* (New York: Oxford University Press).

van Agtmael, Antoine W. (1984), *Emerging Securities Markets: Investment Banking opportunities in the developing world* (London: Euromoney Publications).

White, Gordon (1987), 'The Politics of Economic Reform in Chinese Industry: The Introduction of the Labour Contract System', *The China Quarterly*, no. 111 (September).

World Bank (1988), *China: Finance and Investment*, A World Bank Country Study (Washington DC: The World Bank).

—— (1985), *China: long term development issues and options* (Baltimore: The Johns Hopkins University Press).

Xu, Jing'an (1988), 'The Stock-Share System: A New Avenue for China's Economic Reform', in *CER*.

Young, Arthur N. (1971), *China's Nation-Building Economic Record* (New York: Hoover Institution Press).

Zhou Xiaochuan and Zhu Li (1988), 'China's Banking System: Current Status, Perspective on Reform', in *CER*, pp. 399–409.

Zuo Mo (1987), 'An Exploration into Several Problems Related to the Restructuring of the System of Ownership', *Chinese Economic Studies*, vol. 20, no. 3 (Spring).

Restructuring the Rouble: Prospects for Convertibility

SPECIAL MERIT AWARD

Editors' Introduction

Foreign investors in the Soviet Union hoping for rouble convertibility any time soon will be disappointed, argue Stephen Gardner and Steven Green of Baylor University. Indeed, convertibility of the rouble at this stage in the Soviet Union's economic reform programme would have disastrous effects. Some Soviet and western observers have called for immediate removal of all price, quantity, and currency restrictions, and others have advocated the introduction of a 'two-tiered' market for foreign exchange, but a step-by-step approach to reform has the best chance of succeeding. The authors caution, however, that is important for Soviet leaders to undertake reforms in the proper sequence. The first step is to stabilize the economy, which requires a reduction in the government's deficit. This means that government enterprises can no longer sustain large operating losses. It is also important to offer viable alternatives to currency hoarding, because the large stocks of roubles now held by consumers would pose a large inflation threat if prices were allowed to move with market conditions. The Soviet culture must also make difficult adjustments with the introduction of market institutions into the economy. The essay concludes that, given the size of the changes needed as a prerequisite, it is unlikely that rouble convertibility will happen any time soon. The very factors that work against convertibility, however, 'will also create substantial profit opportunities for firms clever enough to anticipate them'.

H. Stephen Gardner, 38, is the Ben H. Williams Professor of Economics, Hankamer School of Business, Baylor University, Waco, Texas. He holds a Ph.D. from the University of California, Berkeley, and has conducted research in the USSR as a guest of the Soviet Academy of Sciences. He is the author of two books—*Soviet Foreign Trade: The Decision Process* (1983) and *Comparative Economic Systems* (1988)—and articles in numerous publications including *Comparative Economic Studies* and *The Columbia Journal of World Business*.

Steven L. Green, 32, is Associate Professor of Economics, Hankamer School of Business, Baylor University, Waco, Texas. He holds a Ph.D. from Brown University and has held positions at Vanderbilt University, the Federal Reserve Bank of Dallas, and the Economics Institute in Boulder, Colorado. His publications include articles in the *Journal of Monetary Economics* and the *Journal of Economic Development*. His primary research interests are in the areas of monetary policy and inflation.

11

Restructuring the Rouble: Prospects for Convertibility

H. STEPHEN GARDNER AND STEVEN L. GREEN

> We create fairy tales about the future, supposing that if
> we provide unlimited opportunities for the use of [market]
> relations, His Majesty the rouble will do everything else, and
> tomorrow we will have a land of prosperity.
>
> Mikhail Antonov, Soviet sociologist,
> to the Russian Republic Writer's Union,
> December 1988

In January 1987 the Soviet government opened the door to foreign participation in joint ventures on their territory. By mid-1989, some 680 ventures were registered, and hundreds of others were under negotiation. Most of these projects are very small, with an average foreign investment of only $2 million.

New foreign partners to joint ventures in the Soviet Union quickly realize that they must participate in barter transactions or other complex arrangements to repatriate their rouble profits—that is, to convert their roubles into hard currency and bring them home. This inconvertibility problem is one of the most important obstacles to expansion of the Soviet joint venture program. The inconvertibility of the rouble is a symptom, in turn, of rigid price controls, central planning, commodity shortages, and arbitrary exchange rates. Soviet prices do not reflect domestic supply-and-demand conditions or international values. If the Soviets were to move the rouble significantly toward conventional notions of convertibility, their economy would suffer an enormous deficit in its international payments, quickly exhausting their currency reserves.

For these and other reasons, the rouble will remain isolated from world currency markets until the next century. Foreign firms operating in the Soviet Union must confront and endure the inconvertibility problem; it will not soon disappear. Ironically, rouble inconvertibility also offers profit-making opportunities to financial intermediaries and trading firms that facilitate the Soviet transition to a market culture.

The Meaning of 'Convertibility'

All but a handful of the world's currencies carry some restrictions on when they can be legally traded for other currencies. These restrictions usually involve one or both of the following: (i) whether the transaction is associated with economic activities deemed desirable by the authorities, and (ii) whether the parties undertaking the transaction are residents or non-residents.

Regarding the class of desirable activities, analysts focus on the distinction between current account and capital account con-vertibility. Currencies are often fully convertible for purposes of current account activity (involving payment for goods, services, or unilateral transfers) but not fully convertible for capital account activity (involving the transfer of debt or equity). According to the International Monetary Fund, at the end of 1987, sixty-five of its 147 members had full current account convertibility, but only thirty had full capital account convertibility.

Convertibility may also depend on residency status. Quite often, nonresidents are able to trade in foreign currency for a broader class of current and/or capital account activities than residents. The liberalization of foreign exchange markets often begins with the extension of current-account convertibility to nonresidents.

The convertibility issue therefore involves the class of activities for which a currency may be legally exchanged for other currencies. The specific issue of concern to foreign firms in the Soviet Union is when they will be able—directly or indirectly—to convert their rouble-denominated profits into hard currency. Soviet leaders are almost unanimous in their desire to ease convertibility restrictions, but they are uncertain about the best way to pursue this goal.

Three Approaches to Rouble Convertibility

The most direct approach to the inconvertibility problem would be a 'Big Bang': all price, production, and exchange controls would be removed simultaneously, and economic activities would be directed by markets. This is the approach suggested by many Western observers, but it has been accepted by very few Soviet analysts. At the present time a Big Bang is precluded by growing budget deficits, inflationary financing, weak instruments of monetary control, shortages of consumer goods, and the consequent 'rouble overhang'. Soviet economists fear that immediate decontrol of prices would unleash an unrestrained hyperinflation, complicating all of the other financial reforms. For example, Rabkina and Rimashevskaia maintain that 'whoever believes . . . [the scarcity problem] is unsolvable with the present state of prices should realize that under conditions of runaway inflation . . . we would proceed from a difficult task to an impossible task'.

More importantly, deregulation of prices woud threaten the political viability of the entire program of *perestroika*. Price control, with subsidies for food, housing, and other necessities, is presently one of the/pillars of the nation's social welfare system. Soviet officials are perfectly aware of the political fall-out from runaway inflation in China, Poland, and Yugoslavia.

A second approach to convertibility, the so-called 'Two-Track' model, is suggested by Soviet experience during the early 1920s. Beginning in 1922, a monetary reform was conducted to create a stable currency for Lenin's market-oriented New Economic Policy. The State Bank was authorized to issue a new bank note, the *chervonets*, which was partially backed by gold but not convertible into gold. At the same time, the old paper rouble, printed to finance budget deficits, was left in circulation, and it depreciated rapidly against the *chervonets*.

The governmental budget was drawn into balance during 1923–4, making it possible to eliminate the old paper rouble. This made it possible to establish the *chervonets* as the sole currency in 1924, when it was exchanged for old roubles at a rate of 1 : 150,000. The new stabilized currency put an end to barter arrangements that accompanied the hyperinflation of the early 1920s. For a short time the *chervonets* was quoted on foreign exchange markets.

Sokolnikov, the Finance Commissar who engineered the monetary reform, was rewarded by Lenin with a position on the Politburo. Later, he opposed Stalin's program of rapid industrialization financed with paper money, and he paid for that opposition with his life. Today, Sokolnikov is a cult hero in the economic folklore of *perestroika*.

Several influential Soviet economists, including Abel Aganbegyan and Oleg Bogomolov, have recently proposed a similar program of monetary reform. They would introduce a new currency convertible into gold and energy supplies, allowing it to circulate alongside the paper rouble. Apparently, this convertibility would be available only to nonresidents for current account transactions. The currency would be unified only after the fiscal and monetary system is stabilized, as in 1924.

The Two-Track approach is attractive because it promises rapid progress toward partial convertibility, but it is inappropriate for an economy fettered by a monolithic system of central planning, price controls, and subsidies. The convertible *chervonets* was a natural component of Lenin's New Economic Policy, with its strong reliance on markets. Prime Minister Ryzhkov has rightly observed that the Two-Track model is 'somewhat artificial' and could breed 'considerable social tension' under the current system of central planning. Introduction of a new monetary asset is no substitute for true economic reform.

The Gorbachev administration favours a 'Step-By-Step' approach to rouble convertibility. First, the country's financial house must be put in order with a series of fiscal, monetary, structural, and social-welfare reforms. During this stage, minor adjustments will also be made in the system of wholesale prices, and limited auctions will be conducted to allocate foreign exchange, but retail prices will be left untouched. In the second stage, wholesale and retail price controls will be lifted gradually, and wages will be adjusted to compensate the public for any loss of real income. Finally, after financial equilibrium and a flexible system of domestic prices have been established, additional steps will be taken toward current-account convertibility for residents and nonresidents. According to official pronouncements, this entire process cannot be completed in less than a decade, and that is probably an optimistic assessment.

This cautious Step-By-Step approach to liberalization may not be attractive to free-market economists, and it may be overtaken by inertia, but it provides the most realistic scenario for Soviet reform in the near future. The short-term adjustment costs associated with a Big Bang are politically unacceptable, and the Two-Track approach is viable only after fundamental structural problems have been addressed.

Economic theory and the experiences of other countries suggest that the success or failure of the Step-By-Step approach will depend in part on the sequence of liberalization. Theory suggests that a poorly-ordered liberalization of markets can actually cause economic performance to deteriorate. For example, the government may decontrol the costs of a group of firms without decontrolling revenues. The resulting financial distress can have adverse consequences for the entire economy.

Successful programs of financial liberalization have usually begun with stabilization of fiscal and monetary policy and then advanced from reform of domestic product markets to liberalization of markets for capital and foreign exchange. The World Bank's 1989 *World Development Report* finds that 'reforms carried out against an unstable macroeconomic background [resulting from large budget deficits and rapid money growth, for example] can make that instability worse' and that 'financial liberalization may not improve the allocation of resources'. These findings suggest that the first major step on the road to rouble convertibility should be stabilization of the Soviet domestic economy.

Requirements for Domestic Stabilization

The most important obstacle to stabilization of the Soviet economy is the so-called 'rouble overhang'—the fact that too many roubles are chasing too few consumer goods. We cannot measure the magnitude of this problem because the Soviet government does not publish comprehensive money supply data, but Prime Minister Ryzhkov places the 'unsatisfied demand' for consumer goods at about 90 billion roubles in 1988, or 20 per cent of total consumer purchases of goods and services. Some Soviet economists speak of an overhang as large as 500 billion roubles. At any rate, the importance of this problem is beyond question.

In its program to eliminate the rouble overhang, the Soviet government must fight on several fronts. First, it must set its own accounts in order. In 1989, the governmental deficit will be about 120 billion roubles, financed largely with the printing press. Finance Minister Pavlov claims that the deficit will be halved in 1990, but this is probably wishful thinking. Over a period of several years, in concert with the general economic reform, deficit reduction should be accomplished by eliminating subsidies to money losing enterprises, by reductions in military spending, and by a host of other fiscal measures. According to official pronouncements, defence spending will be reduced by 10 billion roubles, or about 14 per cent, in 1990–1, and by 33–50 per cent by 1995.

Second, any enhancement of enterprise autonomy must be accompanied by stronger market discipline. Soviet enterprises unencumbered by concern with profits used bank loans to raise their workers' wages by about 8 per cent in 1988 and 10 per cent (over the previous year) in the first half of 1989—far ahead of labour productivity. The rapid growth in money incomes, financed by bank credit, only added to the rouble overhang.

Third, the government should absorb part of the overhang by issuing bonds yielding, say, 10 per cent rather than the 3 per cent presently offered by savings banks. The problem here is one of credibility—there may not be a reasonable interest rate that will make rouble bonds more attractive to Soviet citizens than scarce consumer goods.

Finally, elimination of the rouble overhang will require a profound structural adjustment of the Soviet economy. Abel Aganbegyan speaks of the need to 'flood the market with consumer goods'. He believes that 20 billion roubles could be removed from the economy each year by increasing construction of housing, and by selling one-third of the new residences to their occupants. He would enlist the aid of foreign capital to increase automobile, consumer electronics, and personal computer production, absorbing another 35 billion roubles. Finally, he would double the volume of consumer goods imports in the next few years, yielding another 10 billion roubles.

Some aspects of the Aganbegyan plan have already been adopted by the government. According to recent revisions of the official economic plan for 1990, centralized capital investment will be cut by about 30 per cent, and the freed resources will be devoted to a 12 per cent expansion of consumer goods production. Already, several defence and industrial plants have been converted to produce consumer goods. A giant tractor complex that was under construction has been converted to produce 900,000 compact cars per year. The share of civilian products in the total output of the defense industry is scheduled to increase from 40 per cent currently to 50 per cent in 1990 and to some 60 per cent by 1995.

Martin Feldstein has argued that there is a 'fundamental

confusion' involved in trying to reduce the overhang by increasing consumer goods production, because the 'roubles paid by consumers would simply be transferred to the workers and enterprises that produced the goods, resulting in no reduction in the stock of roubles'. Evidently, Feldstein has forgotten to adjust his analysis for a fully employed economy. Increasing production of consumer goods *in place of* producer goods will not create any appreciable increase in aggregate income or money emission. The same stock of roubles will chase a larger volume of consumer goods.

Interestingly, the need for structural adjustment was explained cogently by Lev Shanin in 1925. In his essay, 'The Economic Nature of Our Commodity Shortage', Shanin argued for a shift in investment priorities from heavy industry to consumer-goods production:

> The illusion prevails in our country that all that has to be done to overcome the commodity-shortage crisis is to develop the industrial machine to the utmost . . . We must realize that the heavy industries can be developed only on the basis of extensive preliminary development of light industry (or importation of consumers' goods), i.e., only provided light industry is in a position to make available the . . . supplies of commodities needed to satisfy the consumers' demand created by the development of heavy industry.

Reform should therefore begin with the stabilization of fiscal and monetary policy, but effective policy reforms can only be undertaken if there is sufficient political support. Such support can be gained only if Soviet leaders pay close attention to the composition of output—specifically, the fraction of output devoted to consumer goods production—and its distribution. If this initial stage of the liberalization process is successful, the next stage should be the reform of domestic product markets. In the Soviet case, this means the adoption of prices as the primarily allocation mechanisms. For this aspect of the program to succeed, however, the Soviets must develop a market culture.

Creating a Market Culture

Western observers sometimes forget that a market economy involves more than just buying and selling at prices that move in response to changes in supply and demand. The nitty-gritty aspects of market transactions are so institutionalized in the West that they are taken for granted, but this is not the case in the Soviet Union. The prerequisites for price reform described above are necessary for *perestroika* to succeed, but not sufficient. Soviet citizens must also be able to use their new economic freedoms effectively.

It may seem that teaching rational, self-interested humans how to undertake market transactions is no more necessary than teaching birds in the northern hemisphere how to fly south for the winter. This view is overly simplistic. An aggressive young person needs more than rational self-interest to become an investment banker; he or she also needs training in economics and finance. Soviet citizens, who have no cultural tradition of pervasive market institutions, need a better understanding of all facets of market behaviour.

The introduction of market mechanisms into the Soviet economy is already causing a profound culture shock. Soviet citizens will eventually be required to make major adjustments in their day-to-day lives. Price reform and *perestroika* will be accompanied by fear and resentment. Even if the changes are beneficial economically, the substantive change will create social unrest.

Consider some of the aspects of economic life that Westerners view as normal: searching for a job; negotiating a lease; buying health, property, and disability insurance; saving for retirement; balancing a bank statement; filing tax returns; borrowing money to purchase a car or house; moving to a far-away location to take advantage of a good job opportunity; settling an estate after the death of a relative; asking one's supervisor for a higher salary; paying union or association dues; filing for bankruptcy; closing a real estate transaction; purchasing equity shares or long-term bonds; securing financing to start a new business; hiring and firing workers; dealing with suppliers; managing inventory; and so on.

Soviet citizens have little or no experience with these or the thousands of other activities that are a normal part of life in a market economy. Faced with the prospect of doing these things for themselves, many Soviet citizens will express a preference for queueing. They will be reluctant to trade the familiar for the unknown.

Although some Western advocates of rapid price reform may not appreciate these realities, Soviet leaders certainly do. The slow pace of reform policies to date reflects this understanding, as well as the political concerns that are usually emphasized.

Western investors should not bank on the emergence of a convertible rouble any time in the near future. How, then, should they approach investment in the Soviet Union? Western firms will find many profit opportunities in helping the Soviet people acquire market-related skills.

As a specific example, consider the rouble repatriation problem. Suppose a Western firm engages in a joint venture that successfully cracks the Soviet market and is very profitable. The firm would like to convert its rouble-denominated profits into dollars, but the absence of a market for foreign exchange prohibits it from doing so directly. Instead, it must incur substantial transactions costs to make the conversion, perhaps by bartering for exportable goods. Many foreign firms in the Soviet Union face this problem, and it is not likely to go away in the near future. Here is a clear role for a financial intermediary that solves repatriation problems by matching firms more cheaply than the firms can find one another.

The market for this particular intermediation service would end when (if) rouble convertibility is established for nonresident current-account activities. The intermediary should recognize this fact when it enters the market and plan for the day when its repatriation services will no longer be needed. In this example, the liberalization of domestic financial markets that will accompany rouble convertibility will create other intermediation opportunities.

More generally, foreign firms should be able to find many lucrative opportunities involving the development of a market culture in the Soviet Union. As free markets develop, transactions costs will initially be very high, and firms that find ways to reduce transactions costs will be quite profitable.

Summary and Conclusions

Western investors involved with the Soviets in joint ventures long for a convertible rouble, and Western economists are prodding the Soviet Union to move more quickly toward market mechanisms. Both groups will be disappointed, because a premature move to rouble convertibility would have disastrous consequences for the Soviet economy. These consequences could include large payments deficits, hyperinflation, the abandonment of *perestroika*, increased repression in domestic policies and paranoia in foreign policies, and a Soviet market closed to Western investors.

The Soviet leaders are wise to take a cautious approach to economic restructuring, and their decision to do so is based primarily on political considerations. This course of action is also consistent with economic theory and history, which suggest that the sequence of policy actions can be an important factor in the success or failure of a liberalization program.

Western firms involved in the Soviet Union, and firms contemplating such involvement, should not expect the rouble to become convertible—even for nonresident current-account activities—for at least a decade. The factors prohibiting rouble convertibility, however, will also create substantial profit opportunities for firms clever enough to anticipate them. Forward-looking firms will recognize the short-term nature of these opportunities and plan to alter their focus when the rouble does become convertible.